The Earl
Christian

The Earliest Christian Text

1 Thessalonians

Gerd Lüdemann

Revised and expanded from the original German

POLEBRIDGE PRESS
Salem, Oregon

Cover and interior design by Robaire Ream

Library of Congress Cataloging-in-Publication Data
Lüdemann, Gerd.
  [Alteste christliche Text. English]
  The earliest Christian text : 1 Thessalonians / by Gerd Lüdemann.
    pages cm
  "Revised and expanded from the German original."
  Includes bibliographical references and index.
  ISBN 978-1-59815-133-6 (alk. paper)
  1. Bible. Thessalonians, 1st--Criticism, interpretation, etc. I. Title.
  BS2725.52.L839513 2013
  227'.81077--dc23
                                                                    2013030934

Contents

Preface

The present work continues my attempts to provide reliable information about Early Christianity. Just as people are interested to learn about the latest discoveries in medical science, so they should, I think, be afforded an equal opportunity to be informed about recent findings in the area of Early Christianity.

This book deals with 1 Thessalonians, a document that most scholars consider to be the earliest extant Christian writing, a judgment I believe to be well founded.

The textual basis of my translations is the critical edition of *Novum Testamentum Graece* by Nestle-Aland, 27th edition. Unless otherwise indicated, all translations are my own. I use the traditional names for the gospels—Matthew, Mark, Luke, and John—though we do not know the identity of their authors.

Following a model quite different from my own, a team of Fellows of the Westar Institute have published a new edition of Paul's authentic letters.* As their Introduction states, "We have not settled for the traditional ways of translating the material. We listened to Paul as he echoed around the Mediterranean" (p. 5). Rather than attempt

> to create a new Paul . . . we have tried to translate Paul dynamically. We do not present a literal, wooden reading. We aim to express what Paul meant in clear North American English. We have sought a dynamic equivalence of Greek to English in order to communicate the meaning Paul wanted to convey. This means that we have not rested comfortably with a word for word strategy. At times we have had to spell out what was implied in Paul's rhetoric. We have tried to find in English ways of conveying Paul's intent. (p. 6)

By way of demurral, I propose that a translation can remain close to the original without being wooden, and that the translator's aim must always be to render faithfully what the author meant. I am glad that my Westar colleagues agree with me on the latter point, and hope only that in spite of dissimilar approaches and wording, our translations might succeed in supplementing each other.

*Dewey et al., *The Authentic Letters of Paul.*

Before the interpretation, I offer an English translation that is both readily intelligible and true to the meaning of the original Greek text. In order to focus attention on the text, I have eliminated the usual captions and headlines and have retained only chapter and verse numerations. Besides, I have italicized and bracketed the Greek words or phrases represented by various English terms and translated all citations from German texts into English.

Three appendices have been included in an attempt to relieve the primary exposition of less-than-essential details and at the same time provide useful supplementary information on various issues that are crucial to a clear understanding of the text and of this book.

Elements of this book appeared in my recent German publication, *Der älteste christliche Text. Erster Thessalonicherbrief.* Springe: zu Klampen, 2012; but that text has undergone such a major expansion, restructuring, and revision that the present book is indeed a new volume.

I thank my Vanderbilt colleague and neighbor Eugene TeSelle for a critical look at the manuscript. My friend Tom Hall has discussed the whole book with me. It owes a great deal to his generous sharing of ideas.

Gerd Lüdemann

Abbreviations

1,2 Chron	1,2 Chronicles
1,2 Cor	1,2 Corinthians
1 Hen	Ethiopic Enoch
1,2 Kgs	1,2 Kings
1,2,3,4 Macc	1,2,3,4 Maccabees
1,2 Pet	1,2 Peter
1,2 Sam	1,2 Samuel
1,2 Thess	1,2 Thessalonians
Bar	Baruch
2 Bar	Syriac Baruch
Col	Colossians
Dan	Daniel
Deut	Deuteronomy
Esth	Esther
Exod	Exodus
Ezek	Ezekiel
Gal	Galatians
Heb	Hebrews
Hos	Hosea
Isa	Isaiah
Jas	James
Jdt	Judith
Jer	Jeremiah
Josh	Joshua
Judg	Judges
Lev	Leviticus
Lk	Luke
LXX	Septuagint (Greek translation of the Hebrew Scriptures)
Matt	Matthew
Mic	Micah
Mk	Mark
Nah	Nahum
Neh	Nehemiah
Phil	Philippians

Phlm	Philemon
Prov	Proverbs
Ps(s)	Psalm(s)
Rom	Romans
Sir	Sirach
TestBenj	Testament of Benjamin
TestLev	Testament of Levi
Tob	Tobit
Wis	Wisdom of Solomon
Zech	Zechariah

Chapter 1

Understanding Paul

THE FOUNDER OF THE COMMUNITY AND THE MISSIONARY

First Thessalonians is a cordial letter from Paul to a recently founded community, but also one in which the apostle uses all his skill and charm to induce the Thessalonians to take his message to heart. Nothing was more important to him than that the Thessalonians should be persuaded of his love, his longing, and his concern for them. For in a very real sense he and they were inseparably united, and every aspect of their relationship reflects a reciprocal giving and taking.

The letter also illustrates Paul's pastoral side.[1] The apostle has skillfully deployed his co-worker Timothy to inform him about the situation at Thessalonica, and now he offers his counsel, and with both overflowing empathy and firm insistence reminds his young community of the rules of conduct and faith he had transmitted to them during the founding visit.

Paul considered his own preaching to be God's word and praised the Thessalonians for accepting it as such. He even stood up to the Roman Empire by periodically appropriating its slogan "peace and security,"[2] and then predicting its total destruction in the near future. In 1 Thess 1:1 we see an unmistakable act of political resistance, for he suggestively identifies the Thessalonian community he had founded as the *ekklêsia* of Thessalonians—a term we translate as "church," but the primary meaning of which was "civic assembly." It was a good thing for Paul that no Roman authority took notice of this.

Despite the harmonious tone, 1 Thessalonians is a "fire letter."[3] Viewing it as a whole, we can see that in it Paul looks into the future more than in any other of his preserved epistles. He expects the second coming of Jesus to happen during his own lifetime and threatens all non-believers—Gentiles and Jews alike—with the certainty of condign judgment. On the other hand, he assures the Thessalonians of their faith and its guarantee of salvation, for unlike the two aforementioned groups they had accepted the gospel message that would save them from the imminent wrath of God.

Of course, Paul tried to establish and solidify his contact with other people, for he confesses a compulsion to preach the gospel.[4] And though he was an effective promoter of a new and very different message, this message no doubt struck most of his audience as not only radical, but indeed exotic. Still, Paul considered the needs of his hearers and was willing to meet them halfway. He openly avows that to the Jews he became a Jew and to the Gentiles, a Gentile.[5] Yet he himself was neither a real Jew nor a real Gentile, and in this, his earliest letter, he even played the part of a popular philosopher.

Paul used every means at his disposal so that he "might save some."[6] "He was an eminent man of action; of powerful soul, progressive enthusiastic; a conqueror, a missionary, a propagator."[7] Paul's burning commitment to the gospel and his apostleship meant that throughout his public life he displayed both a streak of arrogance and a tendency to vacillate. No doubt some were perplexed, but his accomplishments suggest that this adaptability was a good way to succeed.

Gentile Christian communities to whom he introduced the gospel (Philippi and Thessalonica are two good examples) served as bases for his missionary work of proclaiming both the one God of the Jews and Jesus Christ the future savior whom God had raised from the dead. Indeed, he felt called to make Gentiles revere the God of Israel.[8]

His preaching in the newly founded congregations included Jewish teachings of sanctified living that both affirmed the validity of specific parts of the Law in the form of a catechism and reminded spiritually inclined Christians of their duties in daily life. And while from the very beginning circumcision was not practiced, Paul introduced baptism and the Lord's Supper as Christian variations of rites that were at home in mystery religions familiar to all. It is interesting to note that he does not explicitly mention any of these practices in 1 Thessalonians.[9]

THE APOSTLE AND HIS VISION
OF A NEW HUMANITY

Paul regarded himself as the agent of Jesus Christ, called by God and committed to God's cause. Along with his risen Lord he claimed to be part of a cosmic drama under the direction of God almighty. He did not consider the life of Jesus of Nazareth to be an important topic. Paul never met Jesus personally and had little familiarity with his deeds and teachings. In short, he cared but little about the itinerant preacher from Galilee; it was the risen, heavenly Lord that mattered above all else, yet only as the crucified One whose death offered atonement to humankind.[10]

We encounter in Paul a tremendous degree of self-consciousness and self-importance; his emphatic statement that he was superior to many of his contemporaries in observing the law[11] is not only a reflection of his Pharisaic sense of superiority, but also has a basis in his character; as a Christian he would later say of himself that he worked more than all the other apostles,[12] or spoke in tongues more than all the Corinthians together.[13]

Thus as a Christian, his fanaticism merely changed its focus.[14] "Though the call to be an apostle had reversed the direction of his life, Paul in many ways remained the same."[15] If Paul's conversion and ongoing dedication to Christianity had granted him the authority to do so, he would certainly have undertaken harsh retaliatory measures against the Jewish Christians who sought to undermine and disrupt his missionary efforts.[16]

It comes as no surprise that Paul dominated his communities by insisting on his wishes and authority and requiring the compliance of others. His claims of apostolic authority reinforced his sense of infallibility and often led him to bully any who disagreed. As one would expect, he thus gained devoted followers among docile members but also repelled many who were not easily swayed.[17]

Why, then, did Paul seek to eradicate Christianity? It might seem that his fanaticism sprang from the exclusivist conviction that this new sect sullied God's honor and abrogated the divinely enjoined purity of the Jewish community. Such a challenge to God's supremacy would have to be eradicated. But such a view makes it difficult to understand the *sudden* change from persecutor to preacher, especially since the about-face involved a debilitating emotional and physical breakdown.

What is more probable is that basic elements of the preaching of Christians had a strong subconscious influence on Paul. In that case he could well have become a persecutor in order to silence his own self-accusations.

His acquaintance with Christian practice and preaching surely took place at both cognitive and precognitive levels—as is probably true of all social and religious experiences. The explanation suggests itself that Paul's vehement rejection of Christians and his aggressive attitude towards them was based on an inner tension in his person, one of the kind that numerous studies in depth-psychology have identified in other cases as a motivation of aggressive behavior. Is it too much to suggest that the basic elements of Christian practice and preaching subconsciously attracted Paul? Or that fearing his hidden strivings in this direction, he projected these onto Christians so that he could attack them all the more intemperately? Perhaps Paul hated Christians because deep in his heart he hated himself.

But his calling as a Pharisee collapsed unexpectedly. Paul is one of those people whose life is bifurcated by a single inner disaster. Paul had loathed Jesus as a sham messiah and battled against his disciples, but near Damascus in the middle of a persecution that he himself had initiated, he "saw" Jesus in his heavenly glory and heard himself called to be the apostle to the Gentiles. This vision of "God's Son" determined his future life.

From now on his special commission, assigned him by God almighty, was to bring the gospel to the Gentiles in order to inform them that from then on they were included in God's plan of salvation. They did not have to become Jews first, and even though not circumcised, they could obtain the same status as Jews. Henceforth the two groups would belong equally to the church, for together they comprised the new Israel and had become one in Christ; and accordingly they ate with one another, dispensing with Jewish dietary and purity laws: gone was the distinction between clean and unclean.[18]

This praxis had a dynamic of its own and prompted the claim of the church universal that all differences of gender, religion, and status were eliminated. "In denying Jewish privilege as the elect of God, Paul makes the church in theory universal."[19] In Christ all converts were inaugurated into a "new reality" where previous differences of ethnicity, gender, and social condition were replaced or transcended once and for all. Indeed, Christians claimed that very old and decisive ideals and hopes of the ancient world[20] did come true in their community. They declared the utopian unification of all people in Christ.[21] In this way Paul—though insisting always to have remained a Jew—willy-nilly denies "two pillars common to all forms of Judaism: the election of Israel and faithfulness to the Mosaic law."[22]

No wonder then, that Jewish leaders undertook strong and even violent measures to keep him from pursuing his work. But they were as unsuccessful as Paul the Pharisee had been in attempting to eradicate the Christian community of Damascus.[23] Indeed, the utopian notion of the church universal had already gained many sympathizers from Judaism and paganism alike, and could hardly be stopped. Let me try to explain the dynamics of the nascent church by comparing it to a huge covered kettle full of water at a rolling boil: into the energy generated by a growing number of Jewish disciples poured an influx of Gentile converts, and the kettle boiled over, the hissing and bubbling water creating new channels as it cooled—and new communities composed of both Jews and Gentiles sprang up.

PAUL AND THE PEOPLE OF ISRAEL

In 1 Thessalonians Paul assails the "unbelieving" Jews more sharply than any other Christian in the first two centuries.[24] He uses polemic that stems from both Jewish and pagan sources. The Jewish attacks employ the well-known theme that, having killed the prophets, the Jews deserve God's punishment. The pagan assaults combine a broad spectrum of anti-Semitic stereotypes to claim that the Jews do not please God and are hostile to all other human beings. Thus Paul let Jewish and pagan battering amplify one another and incited Gentile Christians of his own communities against non-Christian Jews.

In ensuing fights with Torah-observing Jewish Christians, Paul maligned his Jewish birth-religion by calling it "dung."[25] Moreover, he slandered his opponents as servants of Satan[26] and in the bitterly sarcastic Gal 5:12 urged those who wanted the Gentile Christians to get circumcised, "Let them cut their own whole thing off!"[27]

More than a decade after the composition of 1 Thessalonians in Corinth and shortly before the third journey to Jerusalem that he undertook as a

Chapter 2

Introduction to
First Thessalonians

I. ENVIRONMENT AND COMMUNITY

During the time of the apostle Paul, Thessalonica was the capital of the Roman province of Macedonia, the seat of the proconsul, and the largest city of the province. In importance it ranked far ahead of the Roman colony of Philippi,[1] the location of Paul's last missionary activity before his arrival at Thessalonica.[2] The Macedonian king Cassander had founded the city in 315 BCE and named it after his wife, a half-sister of Alexander the Great (356–323 BCE).

Archaeological discoveries yield little evidence about the pre-Roman era that ended in 168 BCE when the Roman consul L. Aemilius Paullus defeated King Perseus in Pydna. The one noteworthy exception is the remains of a small Serapis temple that carries more then 70 inscriptions in honor of Isis, Serapis, Osiris, and Dionysos. Thus "the religious landscape of Thessalonica in Paul's time was a mixture of ancient Greek fertility gods like Dionysus, Aphrodite, and Demeter, and more recent redeemer gods associated with the mystery religions."[3]

Isis, the official patroness of Philippi, also had cult sanctuaries in Thessalonica and was worshipped in private homes of the wealthy, too, just as was Christ in the homes of his devotees.[4] In addition, the cult of the Cabiri,[5] imported from the island of Samothrace, attracted the patronage of members of the city's upper classes by the time of Augustus.[6] In "some of its manifestations this cult recalled the violent death of a divine figure with orgiastic dancing and a commemorative meal."[7]

From the standpoint of religious and political history, the cult of the emperor was important and is attested in many ways. Most interesting is a coin from Roman times, its obverse stamped with the head of Julius Caesar wearing a diadem and laurel, and the inscription THEOS (God); its reverse bears the head of Octavian and around it the inscription THESSALONIKEÔN.[8]

Religious exclusivity seems to have been more the exception than the rule, and evidence from the first century CE lacks any direct reference to Jewish life in Thessalonica. "The first certain archaeological evidence of Jews in the city is provided by a sarcophagus inscription from the third century CE."[9]

In Acts 17:1, Luke seems to have invented the existence of a synagogue in the Macedonian capital as he has so many details related to Judaism.[10] He repeatedly blames the Jews for attacks on Paul.[11] Indeed, in the farewell speech to the presbyters of Ephesus at Miletus, Luke has Paul characterize plots of the Jews as something that constantly threatened his missionary work.[12] Yet the antagonists in Thessalonica were not Jews but, according to Paul's own witness in 1 Thess 2:14, the general citizenry of Thessalonica. In any case, Riesner errs when he says, "Paul is probably also thinking of the events in Thessalonica when he accuses the Jews: 'they hinder us from speaking to the Gentiles' (1 Thess. 2:16). . . . The account in Acts [17] is able to illuminate the apostle's experience here and to make his shockingly harsh manner of expression at least historically comprehensible."[13]

Notice should also be taken of the lack of Jewish opposition in Acts 16:11–40 and 17:16–34. Furthermore, in Acts 9:23–24, one other place where we can check the veracity of Luke against the primary witness of Paul's letters, it was not the Jews of Damascus who plotted against the apostle but the ethnarch of Aretas.[14] One is therefore justified in taking a skeptical view of Luke's reports about the Jews as persecutors of Paul and the other Gentile Christians. His schematic generalization of the unbelieving Jews as the principal troublemakers and persecutors involves a distortion of reality.

Thus the Thessalonian congregation contained a substantial proportion of Gentiles. Otherwise Paul would not have addressed the Thessalonians thus: "You turned to God from idols to serve a living and true God."[15] However, Luke gives us the names of two Christians from Thessalonica, Jason[16] and Aristarch,[17] who might have been of Jewish descent. I therefore agree with Jewett's conclusion "that the Thessalonian congregation probably consisted of a handful of Jewish Christians and a large majority of Gentile Christians."[18]

2. AUTHENTICITY

Until the nineteenth century a solid consensus held that the apostle Paul had composed 1 Thessalonians, but in 1845 Ferdinand Christian Baur (1792–1860) became an important advocate of its non-authenticity.[19] His analysis first dealt with the two letters to the Thessalonians[20] and went on to make some general remarks on the "small" letters of Paul, in which category he includes 1 and 2 Thessalonians, Philippians, Ephesians, Colossians and Philemon.[21] Baur's arguments are enumerated below, with counter-arguments.

1. According to Baur the "small" letters of Paul have far less creativity, wealth of thought, and intellectual essence than the four "main letters": Romans, 1 and 2 Corinthians, and Galatians. In his view the small letters do not betray an independent writer, for they are stylistically colorless and lack

assembly in Thessalonica." (On the distinction between *assembly* and *church* see the interpretive note on 1 Thess 1:1b below, 28–29.)

1 Thessalonians exhibits an unusual form. It begins in 1 Thess 1:2–3:10 with an extended thanksgiving in which Paul summarizes his relationship with the Thessalonians and in 3:11–13 closes with a prayer.[44] "Indeed, the progression of thought in the consistent repetition of the 'antithetic' relation between writer and addressees unmistakably characterizes the thanksgiving from beginning to end, i.e. from 1:2–3:13."[45] An admonitory section in 4:1–5:28 comes next. And while all the other Pauline letters have a main body, many find that element missing in 1 Thessalonians: "Thus the conclusion is inevitable that the thanksgiving itself constitutes the main body of 1 Thessalonians."[46]

First Thessalonians "is essentially a pastoral letter. . . . Throughout the letter demonstrates an awareness of the conditions of recent converts . . . with whom he has a cordial relationship."[47] No other letter addresses the hearers as "brothers" in proportion to its length more often than 1 Thessalonians.

No other Pauline letter has so close a proximity in time to the founding of a community as 1 Thessalonians.

In 1 Thessalonians Paul directs against the Jews a sharp literary battering (2:14–16). He combines attacks that originate within the Jewish tradition with accusations of distinctively Gentile origin. The assault against the Jews in this section is thus more intense than in any other New Testament text.[48]

The noun "parousia" occurs in 1 Thessalonians more often than in any other writing of the New Testament.[49] The earliest letter of Paul reflects an imminent hope for the parousia: He expects Christians of the first generation to be alive at the coming of Jesus on the clouds of heaven. In addition, 1 Thessalonians' eager anticipation of Jesus' second coming presupposes an established terminal date, since Paul specifies that at Jesus' return a majority of the faithful will still be alive and a number will have died.

Hostility against the Roman Empire permeates Paul's earliest letter: the apostle expects its immediate destruction. 1 Thess 5:3 is the prophetic reversal of a Roman propaganda slogan, *pax et securitas*.[50]

A number of important Pauline theological terms and phrases do not appear in 1 Thessalonians: justification of humans; God's righteousness; law, works, sin and death as agents of evil; and humanity's fundamentally sinful nature.[51] Nowhere in the letter does Paul *quote* "Scripture";[52] rather we find only scriptural *parallels*:[53] Interestingly, the term "with Christ" refers to future[54] rather than present union.[55] Besides, nowhere does Paul indicate (as he often does in later letters) that the believer suffers with Christ,[56] is buried with him,[57] or is crucified with him.[58] And last but hardly least, in this letter the Spirit is solely related to God,[59] not to Christ.[60]

NOTES

1. In the first century CE Thessalonica had around 30,000 inhabitants, whereas Philippi had only between 5,000 and 10,000. Cf. vom Brocke, *Thessaloniki*, 72.

2. We have no reliable knowledge of Paul's preaching at Amphipolis and Apollonia (cf. Acts 17:1). Luke's "description of the route alone suggests that Paul did not engage in missionary activity in either of the two interim stations" (Riesner, *Period*, 294).

3. Dewey et al., *The Authentic Letters*, 27.

4. Cf. Zeller, *Christus*, 22.

5. Cf. Bowden, *Mystery Cults*, 49–67.

6. On the cults at Thessalonica, cf. Donfried, *Paul, Thessalonica, and Early Christianity*, 21–48.

7. Stambaugh and Balch, *The New Testament*, 157; cf. vom Brocke, *Thessaloniki*, 116–42 ("Religious life of Thessalonica in the 1st century AD").

8. Vom Brocke, *Thessaloniki*, 139.

9. Furnish, *1 Thessalonians*, 26. See further Ascough, *Associations*, 191–212 ("Jewish Communities in Macedonia").

10. Cf. vom Brocke, *Thessaloniki*, 207–33 ("The Jews and Their Synagogue," Acts 17:1b). However, vom Brocke assumes the existence of a small Jewish community and that "the Jewish community in Thessalonica as a congregation in the capital of Macedonia did, as Acts reports (Acts 17:1), possess a synagogue" (231). Yet, as vom Brocke himself points out several times, there is no epigraphical or archaeological evidence for Jewish life in Thessalonica in the first century (211 with n. 18, 230). Flawed is the judgment by Riesner, *Paul's Early Period*, 347: "By no means, however, does the lack hitherto of any evidence from outside the New Testament constitute a reason for doubting the existence of a synagogue during the period of Paul's arrival in Thessalonica."

11. Acts 17:5–9, 13.

12. Acts 20:19.

13. Riesner, *Paul's Early Period*, 353.

14. Cf. 2 Cor 11:32–33.

15. 1 Thess 1:9.

16. Acts 17:15–17; cf. Rom 16:21. Note that "Jason" is a Greek name. Many Jews substituted the Greek name Jason for "Jesus" or "Joshua" (Bauer, *A Greek-English Lexicon*, 369). Vom Brocke, *Thessaloniki*, 238–40, presents further arguments against the thesis that Jason was a Jewish Christian.

17. Acts 20:4; 27:2; cf. Phlm 24. Note that Aristarch is a common name. In addition see the comments of vom Brocke, *Thessaloniki*, 243.

18. Jewett, *The Thessalonian Correspondence*, 119.

19. Baur, *Paulus*. On older contributions to 1 Thessalonians, cf. Crüsemann, *Die pseudepigraphen Briefe* 161–85 ("A Sketch of the History of Research of the Discussion of the Authenticity of 1 Thessalonians").

20. Baur, *Paulus*, vol. 2, 94–97.

21. Baur, *Paulus*, vol. 2, 116–22.

22. Baur, *Paulus*, vol. 2, 94.

23. Bornkamm, *Paul*, 88–96 ("Romans as Paul's Testament"). On Paul's authentic epistles see now Dewey et al., *The Authentic Letters*.

24. Baur, *Paulus*, vol. 2, 367.

25. Crüsemann, *Die pseudepigraphen Briefe* (29–240). However, her analysis of 2 Thessalonians plays only a minor role in the book, extending from 241 to 287.

26. Crüsemann, *Die pseudepigraphen Briefe*, 158.

27. Dibelius, *An die Thessalonicher*, 12.

28. Crüsemann, *Die pseudepigraphen Briefe*, 83.

29. Cf. Furnish, *1 Thessalonians*, 31.

30. Crüsemann, *Die pseudepigraphen Briefe*, 240.

31. See above, 6.

32. Crüsemann, *Die pseudepigraphen Briefe*, 142–48.

33. Crüsemann, *Die pseudepigraphen Briefe*, 148.

34. See "Greco-Roman Popular Philosophy in 1 Thess 2:1–12" (Chapter 4).

35. 1 Cor 9:22 (NRSV).

36. Crüsemann, *Die pseudepigraphen Briefe*, 198.

37. See further the interpretive note on 1 Thess 4:13.

38. Cf. Klein, "Apokalyptische Naherwartung," 249 n. 37.

39. Giesen, *Heilsbotschaft*, 273–74.

40. See "The Jewish Background of 1 Thess 4:16–17" (Chapter 4).

41. Klein, "Apokalyptische Naherwartung," 244–45.

42. Klein, "Apokalyptische Naherwartung," 257.

43. Klein, "Apokalyptische Naherwartung," 253.

44. Cf. von Dobschütz, *Die Thessalonicher-Briefe*, 62.

45. Schubert, *Form and Function of the Pauline Thanksgivings*, 20.

46. Schubert, *Form and Function of the Pauline Thanksgivings*, 26. On the epistolary and rhetorical context of 1 Thessalonians see the survey by Donfried, *Paul, Thessalonica, and Early Christianity*, 166–81. Yet, Schubert remains basic.

47. Malherbe, *The Letters to the Thessalonians*, 78. Jewett, *The Thessalonian Correspondence*, disagrees: 1 Thessalonians "is misunderstood when taken to mean that there are no serious problems in the congregation, that the extended thanksgiving reveals a thoroughly positive, unproblematic situation" (91).

48. See "Traditions in 1 Thess 2:15–16" (Chapter 4).

49. 1 Thess 1:10; 3:13; 4:15; 5:2, 23.

50. *eirênê kai asphaleia*. On this phrase, see the interpretive note on 1 Thess 5:3.

51. For details of Paul's use of these concepts in his other letters see Strecker, *Theology of the New Testament*, 116–56.

52. The other two Pauline letters in which the Apostle does not quote the Old Testament are Philippians and Philemon.

53. Dewey, *The Authentic Letters*, 35, presents the following list: 1 Thess 1:3/4; Macc 17:4; 1 Thess 2:4/Jer 11:20; Prov 17:3; 1 Thess 2:16/Gen 15:16; 1 Thess 3:11/Jdt 12:8 (LXX) 1 Thess 3:13/Zech 14:5; 1 Thess 4:5/Jer 10:25; Ps 79:6; 1 Thess 4:8/Ezek 36:37; 37:14; 1 Thess 4:13/Wis 3:18; 1 Thess 5:1/Wis 8:8; 1 Thess 5:3/Isa 13:8; Jer 6:24; 1 Thess 5:8: Isa 59:17; Wis 5:18; Job 2:9 (LXX). 1 Thess 5:14/Isa 57:15 (LXX)/Prov 14:29 (LXX).

54. Cf. 1 Thess 4:17; 5:10.

55. Cf. Rom 6:8; Gal 2:19; Phil 3:10.
56. Rom 8:17.
57. Rom 6:4.
58. Gal 2:19.
59. 1 Thess 4:8.
60. 1 Cor 15:45; 2 Cor 3:17.

Chapter 3

Translation

1:1Paul, Silvanus, and Timothy

to the assembly of Thessalonians in God the Father and the Lord Jesus Christ:

Grace to you and peace.

2We always thank God for you all, mentioning you in our prayers, constantly 3remembering

your work of faith

and labor of love

and endurance of hope for our Lord Jesus Christ

in the presence of our God and Father. 4We know, brothers beloved by God, that he has chosen you; 5for our gospel came to you not only in words, but also in power and in the Holy Spirit and much conviction. And you know what kind of people we became among you for your sake.

6And you became imitators of us and of the Lord, for you received the word in much affliction, with joy inspired by the Holy Spirit. 7And thus you became an example to all the believers in Macedonia and in Achaia. 8For the word of the Lord has sounded forth from you not only in Macedonia and Achaia, but

---

1:1 *Paul* 2:18. *Timothy* 3:2, 6. *Father* 1:3; 2:11; 3:11, 13. *God* 1:2–3, 4, 8–9; 2:2, 4–5, 8–10, 12–15; 3:2, 9, 11, 13; 4:1, 3; 5:9, 18, 23. *Grace* 5:28. *Peace, be at peace* 5:3, 13, 23.

1:2 *All, always* 1:7; 2:15; 3:7, 9, 12–13; 4:6, 10; 5:5, 14–15, 18, 22. *Thank* 2:13; 3:9; 5:18. *Prayers, pray* 5:17, 25. *Constantly* 2:13; 5:17.

1:3 *Remember* 2:9. *Work* 5:13. *Faith, faithful* 1:8; 3:2, 5–7, 9; 5:8, 24. *Labor* 2:9; 3:5. *Love, beloved* 1:4; 3:6, 12; 4:9–10: 5:8. 13. *Hope* 2:19; 4:13; 5:8. *Lord* 1:8; 3:8, 11–12; 4:1–2, 6, 15–17; 5:2, 9, 12, 27.

1:4 *Brother(s)* 2:1, 9, 14, 17; 3:1, 7; 4:1, 6, 9–10, 13; 5:1, 4,12, 14, 25–27.

1:5 *Gospel* 2:2, 4, 8–9; 3:2. *Holy Spirit* 1:6; 4:8. *Word* 1:6, 8; 2:5, 13; 4:15, 18. *(As) you/we know* 1:4; 2:1–2, 5, 11; 3:3–4; 4:2.

1:6 *Imitator* 2:14. *Affliction* 3:3–4, 7. *Joy, rejoice* 2:19–20; 3:9; 5:16.

1:7 *Macedonia* 1:8; 4:10. *Achaia* 1:8.

your faith in God has gone forth everywhere, so that we need not say anything, [9]for people tell about us and the welcome we found with you, and how

> you turned to God from idols,
> to serve a living and true God,
> [10]and to wait for his Son from heaven,
>
> whom he raised from the dead,
> Jesus, who rescues us
> from the wrath to come.

[2:1]For you yourselves know, brothers, that our welcome among you was not in vain; [2]but though we had already suffered and been mistreated at Philippi, as you know, we expressed ourselves freely in the presence of our God and declared to you the gospel of God in the midst of a great struggle.

[3]For our exhortation (came)

> neither from fraud
> nor from uncleanness,
> nor with deceit;

[4]but just as we have been tested by God to be entrusted with the gospel, so we speak, not to please people but God, who tests our hearts.

[5]For we did not approach you

> with words of flattery,
>   as you know,
> nor with greedy motives,
>   as God is witness,
> [6]nor seeking glory of people
>   either from you or from others,

[7]though as apostles of Christ we could have burdened (you financially). But we were gentle among you, like a nurse taking care of her children.

[8]So, deeply longing for you, we were ready to share with you not only the gospel of God but also our own selves, because you have become very dear to us.

1:9 *Welcome* 2:1.
1:10 *Dead, die* 4:14, 16; 5:10. *Wrath* 2:16; 5:9.
2:1 *In vain* 3:5.
2:2 *Suffer* 2:14.
2:4 *(Not to) please* 2:4, 15; 4:1.
2:6 *Glory* 2:12, 20.
2:7 *Burden, burdened* 2:9. But we were gentle among you, like a nurse taking care of their children. // **2:11** As you know, like a father with his children . . .
2:8 *Longing* 3:6.

⁹For you remember our labor and toil, brothers; we worked night and day, that we might not burden any of you while we preached to you the gospel of God.

¹⁰You are witnesses, and God is, too, of how

> holy,
> righteous
> and blameless

we behaved to you believers. ¹¹As you know, like a father with his children

> ¹²we comforted you
> and encouraged you
> and implored you

to walk in ways worthy of God,

> who calls you into his own kingdom and glory.

¹³And therefore we thank God constantly for the fact that when you received the word of God you heard from us, you accepted it not as a word of people but as what it really is: the word of God, which is also at work in you believers.

¹⁴For you, brothers, became imitators of the churches of God in Christ Jesus that are in Judea; for you suffered the same things from your own compatriots as they did from the Jews,

> ¹⁵who killed both the Lord Jesus
> and the prophets,
> and persecuted us severely,
> and do not please God,
> and oppose all people.

> ¹⁶They prevent us from speaking to the Gentiles
>   that they may be saved,
> and thus fill up the measure of their sins forever.

> But the wrath has come upon them until the end.

¹⁷But we, brothers, at the time in question orphaned from you in person, though not in heart, endeavored the more eagerly and with great desire to see you face to face. ¹⁸For we wanted to come to you—I, Paul, again and again—but Satan hindered us.

¹⁹Who, then, is

2:16 *Come upon/ahead of 4:15.*
2:17 *See you face to face 3:10.*
2:19 *(Second) coming 3:13; 4:15; 5:23.*

> our hope
> or joy
> or crown of boasting

except for you before our Lord Jesus at his coming? [20]You are our glory and joy.

[3:1]Therefore when we could endure it no longer, we resolved to be left behind at Athens alone. [2]And we sent Timothy, our brother and God's fellow-worker in the gospel of Christ, to strengthen and comfort you in your faith [3a]so that no one be shaken by these afflictions.

[3b]You yourselves know that we are destined for this. [4]For when we were with you, we told you beforehand that we were to suffer affliction; and as you know, it has come to pass.

[5]Therefore, when I could endure it no longer, I sent [Timothy] that I might learn of your faith, for fear that somehow the tempter had tempted you and our labor had been in vain.

[6]But now Timothy has come to us from you, and has brought us the good news of your faith and love, and reported that you always remember us kindly and long to see us, just as we long to see you. [7]Therefore, we have been comforted, brothers, because of you in all our distress and affliction through your faith. [8]For now we live, if you stand firm in the Lord.

[9]How can we thank God enough for you, for all the joy in which we rejoice before God for your sake? [10]We pray earnestly night and day that we may see you face to face and complete whatever may be lacking in your faith.

[11]Now may our God and Father, and our Lord Jesus, direct our way to you;

[12]And may the Lord make you increase and excel more and more in love to one another and to all, as we do to you—[13]in order to strengthen your hearts without blame in sanctity before our God and Father at the coming of our Lord Jesus with all his saints.

[4:1]Finally, brothers, we ask and exhort you in the Lord Jesus that just as you received from us how to live and please god, as indeed you are living, so may you excel more and more. [2]For you know what instructions we gave you through the Lord Jesus Christ.

[3]This, then, is the will of God and your sanctification:

> that you abstain from fornication;

> [4]that each of you take for himself a vessel (wife) in sanctification and honor, [5]not in lustful passion like the Gentiles who do not know God;

3:1 *When we/I could endure it no longer 3:5.*
3:12 *Excel more and more 4:1, 10.*
3:13 *Sanctity, saints, sanctification 4:3–4. 7; 5:26.*

⁶that nobody wrong or exploit his brother in your dealings with him.

For the Lord is an avenger in all these things,
    as indeed we have predicted and solemnly affirmed.
⁷For God has not called us to uncleanness but to sanctification.
⁸Therefore whoever disregards this, disregards not people but God, who gives his Holy Spirit to you.

⁹But concerning brotherly love, you do not need to have anyone write to you, for you yourselves have been taught by God to love one another ¹⁰and indeed you do (love) all the brothers throughout Macedonia.

But we urge you, brothers, to excel more and more,

    ¹¹to aspire to live quietly,
    to mind your own affairs, and
    to work with your own hands—as we charged you—

¹²so that you behave properly to outsiders, and become dependent on nobody.

¹³But we do not want you to be ignorant, brothers, concerning those who are asleep, so that you may not grieve like the rest who have no hope.
¹⁴For since we believe that

    Jesus died and rose,

so also God through Jesus will bring with him those who have fallen asleep.
    ¹⁵This we say to you by a word of the Lord:

    that we who are alive, who are left until the Lord's coming,
    shall by no means precede those who have fallen asleep.

¹⁶For the Lord himself will descend from heaven
    with a cry of command,
    with the archangel's call,
    with the sound of the trumpet of God.
And the dead in Christ will rise first;
    ¹⁷then we who are alive, who are left,
    shall be caught up in the clouds together with them
    to meet the Lord in the air;
and so we shall forever be with the Lord.

4:13 *Being/having fallen asleep* 4:14–15. *Like the rest* 5:6.
4:14 *Rise* 4:16.

[18]Therefore comfort each other with these words.

[5:1]But as to the times and dates, brothers, you do not need to have anything written to you.

[2]For you yourselves know full well that the day of the Lord will come like a thief in the night. [3]When people say, "There is peace and security," then sudden destruction will come upon them just as the pain of childbirth [comes] upon a pregnant woman, and they will not escape.

[4]But you, brothers, are not in such darkness that the day could come upon you like a thief;

[5]for all of you are sons of light and sons of the day.

We are not of the night or of darkness, [6]so then let us not sleep like the rest, but let us keep awake and be sober.

[7]For those who sleep, sleep at night;

and those who get drunk, get drunk at night.

[8]But since we belong to the day, let us be sober, and put on the breastplate of faith and love, and as a helmet the hope for salvation.

[9]For God has not destined us for wrath, but to obtain salvation through our Lord Jesus Christ,

[10]who died for us

so that whether we wake or sleep we might live with him.

[11]Therefore comfort each other and build one another up, as indeed you do.

[12]But we ask you, brothers, to respect those

who labor among you
and govern you in the Lord
and admonish you,

[13]and to esteem them very highly in love because of their work.

Be at peace among yourselves.

[14]And we exhort you, brothers,

admonish the disorderly,
encourage the despondent,
help the weak,
be patient with them all.

4:18 *Comfort each other* 5:11.
5:2 *Day (of the Lord)* 5:4–5, 8.
5:8 *Salvation, save* 5:9.

¹⁵See that none of you repays evil (*kakon*) for evil (*kakon*),
but always seek to do good (*agathon*) to one another and to all.

¹⁶Rejoice always,
¹⁷pray constantly,
¹⁸give thanks in all circumstances.

For this is the will of God in Christ Jesus for you.

¹⁹Do not extinguish the Spirit,
²⁰do not spurn prophesying,
²¹but examine everything;
hold fast what is good (*kalon*),
²²abstain from all forms of evil (*ponêron*).

²³May the God of peace himself sanctify you wholly,
May your spirit,
and soul
and body be preserved whole,
blameless at the coming of our Lord Jesus Christ.

²⁴He who calls you is faithful,
and he will also do [this].

²⁵Brothers, pray for us.
²⁶Greet all the brothers with a sacred kiss.
²⁷I adjure you by the Lord that this letter be read to all the brothers.

²⁸The grace of our Lord Jesus Christ be with you.

Chapter 4

Interpretation

METHOD

My interpretation of 1 Thessalonians aims above all to determine Paul's intended message to the Christians in Thessalonica. As an historical work it seeks to return the reader to the time of the apostle Paul, but without recourse to the Holy Spirit—for the Bible as a human document ought not to be rationally assigned such a nonhistorical source. Let me hasten to add that although many modern Christians consider Paul's letters to be addressed to them, this belief should not enter into a critical exegesis of the text.[1] Were it to do so, the exegete might no longer be listening to Paul.[2]

Paul wrote this missive to a specific and recently established community whose members have asked pointed questions and have particular problems. These facts must remain presuppositions of the interpretation, not only because the letter is a continuation of his dialogue with the Christians of Thessalonica, but also because Paul often refers to the content of his teaching when he founded the community. His aim is to remind the community of its Christian basis and to build on the traditions he had transmitted to its members.

But I have not restricted myself to discovering the aims of Paul's oldest writing; after interpreting 1 Thessalonians verse by verse, I also evaluate its content and engage in argument with the author—a dialogue that will remain both sympathetic and in close proximity to the text, lest I seem to impose my opinion on both Paul and the reader.

STRUCTURE OF THE LETTER

1:1	Address
1:2–10	Thanksgiving for the status of the community and assurance of remembrance
2:1–12	Recalling Paul's work in Thessalonica
2:13–16	Thanksgiving for the community's steadfastness under persecution
2:17–3:8	Paul's longing to see the Thessalonians. Sending and return of Timothy

I THESSALONIANS 1:1

Address

[1:1a]Paul, Silvanus, and Timothy
  [1b]to the assembly of Thessalonians [1c]in God the Father and the Lord Jesus
  Christ:
  [1d]Grace to you and peace.

1:1a lists Paul, Silvanus,[3] and Timothy[4] as the senders of the letter. According
to 2 Cor 1:19 they were the first preachers of the gospel in Corinth. However,
I presume that Paul was the *sole author* of 1 Thessalonians, and regard the
apparent inclusion of Silvanus and Timothy under the rubric of "we" to reflect
not a real but an epistolary plural.[5] Moreover, it added to their authority as
"co-founders" of the congregation.

1:1b Paul addresses the assembly (*ekklêsia*) composed of Thessalonians
and wishes them grace (*charis*) and peace (*eirênê*). In contrast to his other
letters, Paul here identifies the addressees in terms of their polity rather than
the location of the community. He writes "to the assembly [composed] of
Thessalonians" rather than "to the assembly in Thessalonica." It is worth noting that despite Paul's shift to church location in subsequent epistles,[6] two
inauthentic Pauline letters follow this early usage.[7]

One should not too readily ascribe a technical *Christian* meaning to the
term *ekklêsia*. In Greek this word designates a political assembly,[8] and that
is what Paul's Hellenistic readers would have taken it to mean. By using the
phrase "*ekklêsia* of Thessalonians" Paul either explicitly or metaphorically
likens the Christian community to an assembly that represents the whole
population of Thessalonica. These Christians—and not the pagan citizens
and administrators—supposedly personify the city of Thessalonica.[9] And yet
on other occasions Paul will adopt Christian terminology and define *ekklêsia*
as "community of God"[10] or "community of Christ."[11] He may have purposely
played with words in addressing the Christians of Thessalonica as *ekklêsia*.

Most scholars agree that early Christians obtained the term *ekklêsia* (in
Hebrew *kehal*) from the Greek translation of the Old Testament.[12] This "indi-

---

1:1 *Paul* 2:18. *Timothy* 3:2, 6. *Father* 1:3; 2:11; 3:11, 13. *God* 1:2, 4, 8–9; 2:2, 4–5, 8–10,
12–15; 3:2, 9, 11, 13; 4:1, 3; 5:9, 18, 23. *Grace* 5:28. *Peace, be at peace* 5:3, 13, 23.

cates the parallelism between the church and the people of God on Sinai. The church uses it to say that in the church the hope for the gathering together of Israel has been fulfilled."[13]

1:1c Paul uses the phrase "in God the Father and the Lord Jesus Christ." The phrase "in God"[14] is striking, and calls for explanation. Paul has formed the expression "in God" following the traditional phrase "in Christ."[15] This does not imply "God-mysticism"[16] but is based on what is described by the expression "beloved by God"[17] or "belonging to God."[18] Similarly, "in God" qualifies the phrase "community of the Thessalonians."

1:1d Paul wishes the Thessalonians "grace and peace." In his later letters *charis* is a basic term that connotes a gift and most clearly expresses the occurrence of God's saving deed, his mercy, to human beings.[19] The meaning of *charis* does not always fully reflect Paul's theological teaching of grace, for in the phrase "*charis* be to God"[20] it signifies simply "thanks." Further, Paul designates the collection of money for the Saints in Jerusalem as *charis*.[21] Besides, the related verb *chairô* can serve just as the opening of a Greek letter expressing "greetings."[22]

The use of *charis* in v. 1d ("Grace to you and peace") corresponds to its use in the closing: "The grace (*charis*) of our Lord Jesus Christ be with you."[23] Beyond that, the word *charis* does not occur in 1 Thessalonians. This finding provokes the question of whether before writing this letter Paul had ever used *charis* to express the idea of a gift in the full theological sense.

"Peace" corresponds to the Jewish greeting *shalom* and—used along with *charis*—has a liturgical background. Compare the beginning of a letter in 2 Bar 78:2: "Thus speaks Baruch, the son of Neriah, to the brothers who were carried away in captivity: 'Grace and peace be with you.'"[24]

The brevity of the greeting in v. 1d is striking. In all other authentic epistles of Paul the greeting runs thus: "Grace to you and peace from God, our Father, and the Lord Jesus Christ,"[25] while here we read simply, "Grace to you and peace." The simplicity of the greeting may reflect an early stage of Paul the letter-writer, who had still to develop his own style.

I THESSALONIANS 1:2–10
Thanksgiving for the Status of the Community
and Assurance of Remembrance

²We always thank God for you all, mentioning you in our prayers, constantly ³remembering

---

1:2 *All, always* 1:7; 2:15; 3:7, 9, 12–13; 4:6, 10; 5:5, 14–15, 18, 22. *Thank* 2:13; 3:9; 5:18. *Prayers, pray* 5:17, 25. *Constantly* 2:13; 5:17.

1:3 *Remember* 2:9. *Work* 5:13. *Faith, faithful* 1:8; 3:2, 5–7, 10; 5:8, 24. *Labor* 2:9; 3:5. *Love, beloved* 1:4; 3:6, 12; 4:9–10; 5:8. 13. *Hope* 2:19; 4:13; 5:8. *Lord* 1:8; 3:8, 11–12; 4.1–2, 6, 15–17; 5:2, 9, 12, 27.

> your work of faith
> and labor of love
> and endurance of hope for our Lord Jesus Christ

in the presence of our God and Father.

[4]We know, brothers beloved by God, that he has chosen you, [5a]for our gospel came to you not only in words, but also in power and in the Holy Spirit and much conviction. [5b]So also you know what kind of people we became among you for your sake.

[6]And you became imitators of us and of the Lord, for you received the word in much affliction, with joy inspired by the Holy Spirit. [7]And thus you became an example to all the believers in Macedonia and in Achaia. [8]For the word of the Lord has sounded forth from you not only in Macedonia and Achaia, but your faith in God has gone forth everywhere, so that we need not say anything, [9]for people there tell about us and the welcome we found with you, and how

> you turned to God from idols,
> to serve a living and true God,
> [10a]and to wait for his Son from heaven,
>
> whom he raised from the dead,
> [10b]Jesus, who rescues us
> from the wrath to come.

This section is divided into two parts: vv. 2–5 and vv. 6–10a. The first deals mainly with Paul, the sender of the letter, the second with the community; v. 10b connects the apostle with the community ("us").

As to the form, vv. 2–10 constitute the first part of a thanksgiving to God for the community's perseverance in the faith, a rejoicing that leads Paul in 2:2–12 to add a self-promoting reminder of his work in Thessalonica. In 2:13 ("and therefore we thank God"), Paul begins the second part of the thanksgiving, which ends with 3:8. From 3:9 ("What thanks can we render to God for you . . . ?") to 3:10 Paul adds the third part of the thanksgiving, which in vv. 11–12 concludes with a prayer and the expectation of Jesus' triumphal return.[26]

1:4 *Brothers* 2:1, 9, 14, 17; 3:1, 7; 4:1, 6, 9–10, 13; 5:1, 4,12, 14, 25–27.
1:5 *Gospel* 2:2, 4, 8–9; 3:2. *Holy Spirit* 1:6; 4:8. *Word* 1:6, 8; 2:5, 13; 4:15, 18. *(As) you/we know* 1:4; 2:1–2, 5, 11; 3:3–4; 4:2.
1:6 *Imitator* 2:14. *Affliction* 3:3–4, 7. *Joy, rejoice* 2:19–20; 3:9; 5:16.
1:7 *Macedonia* 1:8; 4:10. *Achaia* 1:8.
1:9 *Welcome* 2:1.
1:10 *Dead, die* 4:14, 16; 5:10. *Wrath* 2:16; 5:9.

1:3 Paul adduces the spiritual strength of the Thessalonians using the words "faith," "love," and "hope," a triad found elsewhere in his letters,[27] and which he here relates to "work," "labor," and "endurance." Thus he stresses that being a Christian involves both effort and specific behavior.[28] In the passages from 1 Thessalonians the order of the triad is in both cases "faith, love, hope" thereby making "hope" central because Paul is waiting for Jesus' return in the near future.

1:4 The address "brothers beloved by God" is striking, for as a rule Paul uses simply "brothers."[29] The repeated use of "brothers" expresses an intimate relationship between Paul and the Thessalonians.[30] Paul certifies their election and apparently assumes a similar understanding on their part. To be sure, the biblical tradition considered Israel as elect,[31] and the rabbis "maintained the biblical attitude of being especially chosen and set aside by God."[32] Thus by using the term "chosen" Paul tacitly degrades "unbelieving" Israel.[33] "Indeed, the appearance of the term *eklogê* with reference to Gentiles is striking in a Pauline letter."[34] The verb "to choose" is equivalent to the verb "to call."[35] The call, of course, is predicated on God's faithfulness,[36] itself a basic biblical term that is connected with election.[37]

1:5 Here Paul recalls his preaching and thus claims a role in conferring on the Thessalonians the "chosen" status mentioned in v. 4. This "election" came about through Paul's preaching of the gospel—"the word"—in concert with "power," the Holy Spirit, and full conviction (one wonders whether the conviction here invoked was Paul's or that of the Thessalonians). In v. 5b, "You know what kind of people we became among you for your sake," Paul invokes not only his own probity, but the fact that the preaching of the gospel and the apostles' personal example while living among the Thessalonians are closely intertwined: that is, he demonstrates the effectiveness of the gospel in his own person. "For the efficacy of the gospel Paul has no other 'proof' but his own appearance among the Thessalonians."[38]

1:6–7 The Thessalonians have become imitators[39] of Paul and of the Lord, and at the same time an example[40] for all Macedonian and Achaian Christians. Phil 3:17 shows that the terms "imitator" and "example" belong together: "Brothers, become my imitators[41] and notice those who so live as you have an example in us."[42]

The theme of imitation is not often found in Paul's letters;[43] in the Old Testament and in Judaism it plays almost no role.[44] Since some scholars understand "imitating" to mean ethical modeling, the logic would run thus: Christians must imitate Jesus and live according to his will. This would echo his call to discipleship in the gospels[45] and correspond to the ethical passages in Paul's letters.[46]

Yet v. 6 goes against such an interpretation, for here imitating Paul and the Lord consists in accepting the word in the context of great affliction that is made bearable by joy in the Holy Spirit. Moreover, in 2:14 the concept of imitation expresses the shared suffering of the Gentile Christians in Thessalonica and the Jewish Christians in Judea. Whether consciously or not, Paul is borrowing motives from mystery religions[47] when he invokes the unity of the Thessalonians, the Jewish Christians in Judea, himself, and Christ.[48] At the same time he probably derived from Jewish traditions the view that election was connected with suffering.[49] Thus in syncretistic fashion, he blended two different ideas.

During the founding of the community Paul had foretold future afflictions,[50] a persecution of Christians that would be a phenomenon of the last times.[51] Like other early Christians[52] he was inspired by the Old Testament book of Daniel[53] to describe the "end times" in detail.[54]

1:8 It is because of the Thessalonians that the word of the Lord, the good news, the gospel, has been heard even beyond Macedonia and Achaia; indeed, the story of the Thessalonians' trust had been told wherever the new faith had been proclaimed. The success of Paul's mission in Thessalonica clearly provided good propaganda. (If one understands the apostle to claim that the news of his success among the Thessalonians has disseminated worldwide rather than to the far reaches of the mission field, then this statement is not merely boastful but demonstrably false.) And the spreading narrative concerns not only the commitment of the Thessalonians, for as the following verse tells us, the apostle's fame increased: people also told stories about Paul's warm reception[55] in Thessalonica.[56]

1:9–10 Verse 9a refers to unspecified persons who tell about Paul and the Thessalonians. Vv. 9b–10 may be part of a pre-Pauline baptismal ritual, for the text contains non-Pauline language and clearly reflects the use of tradition.[57]

The tradition can be divided into two strophes of 3 lines each:

> [9b]You turned to God from idols,
> to serve a living and true God,
> [10a]and to wait for his Son from heaven,
>
> [10b]whom he raised from the dead,
> [10c]Jesus, who rescues us
> from the wrath to come.

In this tradition the ones addressed in v. 9b are united with the speakers in v. 10c. Note the absence of any mention of atonement as the result of Jesus' death.

The first strophe is directed at Gentile Christians who had turned away from idols in order to serve a living and true God, and who are waiting for the Son of God coming from heaven.

The second strophe deals with Jesus raised from the dead and rescuing the Thessalonians from the future wrath. This is reminiscent of John the Baptist's preaching of repentance,[58] which results in escape from "the wrath to come."

I THESSALONIANS 2:1–12

Recalling Paul's Work in Thessalonica

²:¹For you yourselves know, brothers, that our welcome among you was not in vain; ²but though we had already suffered and been mistreated at Philippi, as you know, we expressed ourselves freely in the presence of our God and declared to you the gospel of God in the midst of a great struggle.

³For our exhortation (came)

> neither from fraud,
> nor from uncleanness,
> nor with deceit;

⁴but just as we have been tested by God to be entrusted with the gospel, so we speak, not to please people but God, who tests our hearts.

⁵For we did not approach you

> with words of flattery,
> > as you know,
> nor with greedy motives,
> > as God is witness;
> ⁶nor seeking glory of people,
> > either from you or from others,

⁷though as apostles of Christ we could have burdened (you financially); but we were gentle among you, like a nurse taking care of her children.

⁸So, deeply longing for you, we were ready to share with you not only the gospel of God but also our own selves, because you have become very dear to us.

⁹For you remember our labor and toil, brothers; we worked night and day, that we might not burden any of you, while we preached to you the gospel of God.

¹⁰You are witnesses, and God is, too, of how

> holy,
> righteous,
> and blameless

we behaved to you believers. ¹¹As you know, like a father with his children

---

2:1 *In vain* 3:5.

2:2 *Suffer* 2:14.

2:4 *(Not to) please* 2:4.

2:6 *Glory* 2:12, 20. *Burden, burdened* 2:9.

2:7 But we were gentle among you, like a nurse taking care of their children. // 2:11 As you know, like a father with his children . . .

2:8 *Longing* 3:6.

> [12]we comforted you
> and encouraged you
> and implored you

to walk in ways worthy of God,

> who calls you into his own kingdom and glory.

In this section Paul expands on a topic previously alluded to in 1:5–9, his work in Thessalonica. Having noted in 1:6–8 the gratifying response of the community, he now turns to an account of his missionary work in Thessalonica. Note that the term "welcome" (2:1)—which literally means "entrance"—picks up the same word in 1:9.

2:1 The apostle emphasizes that his coming to Thessalonica was not in vain,[59] and the phrase "you yourselves know"[60] is the first of many reminders that the Thessalonians know him by his deeds,[61] a touting of himself that is repeated throughout the section.[62]

2:2a Paul reports that during the mission in Philippi he suffered hardships and persecution, concerning which Luke offers a more or less credible account and states that the missionaries were accused of introducing non-Roman customs.[63]

2:2b The expression "in the midst of a great struggle"[64] indicates that, as had been the case in the earlier visit to Philippi, Paul's preaching in Thessalonica had involved many difficulties. Nor did Paul's later visits to Philippi go well. Many years later he alludes to it when he says, "You are engaged in the same struggle that you saw I had and now hear that I am having."[65] In both Philippi and Thessalonica apostle and community are involved in similar conflicts.

2:3–4 Because he came to Thessalonica entrusted with the gospel, neither fraud, uncleanness, nor deceit could be ascribed to his mission or his person, the more so since he pleases God and not people.

2:5–6 Like vv. 3–4 this passage lists three negative criteria to show that Paul is judged by divine standards, not human ones.

2:7 For the first and the last time in this letter, Paul claims for himself the designation "apostle" and asserts the consequent prerogative of community support—a right which, as he notes here and in vv. 9–11, he selflessly renounced. Verse 7b emphasizes this point by noting that far from being a burden on the community, he cared for it as would a nurse her own children.

However, Christian missionaries from Jerusalem sent to the Jews[66] had first claimed the privilege of support. They belong to the earliest stage of a mission to the Jews undertaken at the command of the "Risen," who also issued a missionary rule for support of his disciples: "The laborer is worthy of his wages."[67] Paul belongs to the second stage of this movement, which went to the Gentiles. Its members asked for the same right of support as those disciples who turned to the Jews only.

In Corinth around 52 CE Jewish Christian missionaries questioned Paul's apostolic status because he did not receive maintenance from the community. Paul in defense raised three questions:

Do we not have the right to food and drink [from the community]? (1 Cor 9:4)

Do we not have the right to be accompanied by a wife [also supported by the community], as the other apostles and the brothers of the Lord and Cephas? (1 Cor 9:5)

Or is it only I and Barnabas who have no right to refrain from working for a living? (1 Cor 9:6)

Note that more than a decade before his controversies with Jewish Christians in Corinth, Paul had already renounced the right for support from the congregation in Thessalonica. The reason was probably to display veracity in competition with itinerant philosophers there. The controversy over the rights of an apostle heated up much later—after the Jerusalem conference when the legitimacy of Paul's apostleship was discussed.[68] This was of course a situation different from the one in 1 Thessalonians 2. Here, Paul's self-description as apostle is rather general and does not presuppose a polemical context.

2:8–9 Paul brought to the Thessalonians not only the gospel of God but also his love. He reminds them that between preaching the gospel and serving their needs, he has worked day and night.

2:10 This verse introduces the end of the remembrance of his welcome in Thessalonica. Quoting a triad of virtues, Paul describes his demeanor and calls on the Thessalonians and God to be his witnesses.

2:11–12 Verse 12 parallels v. 10 with another triad of virtues that have characterized Paul's life during his stay at Thessalonica. This enables him—as he says in v. 11—to add to his role as nurse (v. 7) that of doting father. An exhortation to walk in ways worthy of God's kingdom rounds off the section.

GRECO-ROMAN POPULAR PHILOSOPHY IN I THESSALONIANS 2:1–12

Martin Dibelius (1888–1947) found numerous parallels between 1 Thessalonians and contemporary popular philosophy,[69] and Abraham J. Malherbe has only recently made further important contributions to this work.[70] In what follows I shall primarily examine a number of parallels to the section under consideration that Malherbe gathered from the discourses of Dio Chrysostomos (ca. 40–120 CE), along with some of Malherbe's interpretive observations.

Let me begin with a comparison of Paul's understanding of his ministry with that of Dio Chrysostomos. The latter writes:

[11]But to find a man who in plain terms and without guile speaks his mind with frankness, and neither for the sake of reputation nor

for gain, but out of good will and concern for his fellow-men stands ready, if need be, to submit to ridicule and to the disorder and the uproar of the mob—to find such a man as that is not easy, but rather the good fortune of a very lucky city, so great is the dearth of noble, independent souls and such the abundance of toadies, mountebanks, and sophists.

[12]In my own case, for instance, I feel that I have chosen that role, not of my own volition, but by the will of some deity. For when divine providence is at work for people, the gods provide, not only good counselors who need no urging, but also words that are appropriate and profitable to the listener. (*Discourses* 32.11–12[71])

Dio's definition of an honorable person and Paul's self-portrait show parallels in both central elements of their self-descriptions and their use of an antithetical presentation ("not . . . but . . ."). To be sure, while Dio was but one among many to boast of exalted personal qualities, selfless concern for others, and a sense of divine calling, Paul's audience surely recognized that his self-description very much echoed that of the ideal philosopher.[72]

2:2–3 The verb "to express oneself freely"[73] appears only here in Paul's letters. In popular philosophy it designates an essential virtue of an orator. Naturally enough, flattery and fraud were regarded as qualities contrary to free expression, and we find Paul renouncing fraud, uncleanness, and deceit.[74] And just as Dio Chrysostom accepts the challenges of life—something other Cynics are supposedly not willing to do[75]—note Paul's emphasis on his struggle in Philippi (v. 2b).

2:4 Like the popular philosophers, Paul feels himself called by God and independent of human beings.[76] The same is true for a Cynic like Epictetus, who distanced himself from fellow Cynics he considered to be deceivers.[77] The expression "to please people" has a rich negative tradition in the rhetoric and ethics of antiquity.[78] Paul uses the verb "to please" in his letters not only positively[79] but also, as in v. 4, negatively.[80] When Paul takes up the charge against sophists and charlatans that they please people, he declares this to be incompatible with someone who has been entrusted with the gospel.

2:5 The noun "flattery"[81] names a standard topic among popular philosophers;[82] it appears only here in the New Testament.

2:6 Paul has not sought popular fame or glory, something that he implies contemporary itinerant teachers seek in order to make money.[83]

2:7 The word "gentle,"[84] which also appears only here in the New Testament, often serves to express the phrase, "showing love for people." It corresponds to the conduct of philosophers who "express themselves freely."

2:9 Renouncing financial support matches the Cynic ideal. "One should endure hardships, and suffer the pains of labor with . . . [one's] own body."[85]

It fits with Paul's claim to be independent, which he describes in a letter to another Macedonian congregation:

> [11]I have learned to be self-sufficient (*autarkês*) in whatever state I am. [12]I know how to be abased, and I know how to abound. In any and all circumstances I have been initiated: plenty and hunger, abundance and want.[86] (Phil 4:11–12)

Koester remarks that Dio's "description of the self-sufficiency (*autarkia*) is in harmony with the[se] Pauline words. . . . According to Dion, passions, desires, and vices are obstacles on the way to morality and self-sufficiency."[87]

2:11–12 Paul's use of the images of father and nurse corresponds to the way popular philosophers were wont to describe their efforts.[88]

But similarities in behavior are not the whole story, for Malherbe detects contrasts between Paul's understanding of God in 1 Thessalonians and that of the popular philosophers. He writes:

> A philosopher would have said that *he* had come, "not in word only, but also in deed." Paul, on the contrary does not draw attention to his accomplishments, but to his gospel which he further describes as the gospel of God (2:2, 9) with which he had been entrusted (2:4), or as the word of the Lord (1:8) or of God (2:13). Furthermore, the gospel came to his readers in the Holy Spirit (1:5) and was received by them with joy of the Spirit (1:6).[89]

Malherbe later continues:

> While the moral philosopher was impelled by an awareness of his own moral freedom, acquired by reason and the application of his own will, to speak boldly to the human condition and demand its reformation, Paul regards his entire ministry, as to its origin, motivation, content, and method, as being directed by God.[90]

Further, Malherbe contrasts the understanding of grief among the popular philosophers with that of Paul:

> Whereas the consolations urge that reason limit the grief lest it become immoderate, for Paul it is the Christian hope, based on Christ's resurrection and coming, that makes comfort possible. The traditions that he uses do not have their origin in the consolations, but the way they are made to function is not foreign to those consolations.[91]

The attitude of Dio Chrysostom to sorrow is well expressed in his sixteenth discourse on pain and distress of spirit. He writes:

> [1]That the majority of us are mastered by pleasure can perhaps be explained: it is because we are under her spell and witchery that

we stay in her company, whereas accepting servitude to pain is
altogether irrational and strange. For although suffering pain and
agony from the severest of all tortures, we nevertheless remain in
it and do not accept the word of reason that frees and delivers us
from our distress. . . . [4]. . . The intelligent person ought not to
feel pain about anything whatever, and be a free person henceforth.
Then there will be release from dread of all that causes distress.
(*Discourses* 16.1.4)

Was the historical Paul really a popular philosopher? Of course not! Above
all, I adduce the differences between Paul and the popular philosophers that
Malherbe so effectively sets forth. We should note two further considerations
that speak unequivocally against the idea that Paul might be counted as a
popular philosopher.

First, Paul both claims and exhibits a mystical relationship to the Christ
who lived in him[92] and in whom he lived.[93] This bond is expressed in the
phrase "in Christ," which has its origin in baptism.[94] It led to Paul's dying and
rising with Christ.[95]

Second, Paul anticipated the return of Jesus during his own lifetime.[96] Along
with all his fellow-believers whether alive or dead, he will supposedly be united
with the Lord at the latter's return.[97]

Since neither of these two understandings could possibly have been found
among the popular philosophers, it is clear that when Paul depicts himself in
terms appropriate to the first-century model of the popular philosopher, his
likely motive is the success of his missionary efforts. As Paul himself points out,
he has "become all things to all people, that I might by all means save some."[98]

Be all that as it may, in view of the congratulations and encomiums heaped
upon the Thessalonians in the first chapter and Paul's repeated self-commen-
dations in this section, one wonders whether a discriminating listener among
the Thessalonians might have sensed a dissonance between these assurances
and the apostle's denial of his use of flattery (v. 5) and eagerness for praise (v. 6).

I THESSALONIANS 2:13–16
Thanksgiving for the Steadfastness of the
Community under Persecution

[13]And therefore we thank God constantly for the fact that when you received
the word of God that you heard from us, you accepted it not as a word of
people but as what it really is: the word of God, which is also at work in you
believers.

[14a]For you, brothers, became imitators of the churches of God in Christ
Jesus that are in Judea; [14b]for you suffered the same things from your own
compatriots [14c]as they did from the Jews,

¹⁵ᵃwho killed both the Lord Jesus	I
¹⁵ᵇand the prophets,	II
¹⁵ᶜand persecuted us severely,	III
¹⁵ᵈand do not please God,	IV
¹⁵ᵉand oppose all people.	V

¹⁶ᵃThey prevent us from speaking to the Gentiles
    that they may be saved,
¹⁶ᵇand thus fill up the measure of their sins forever.

¹⁶ᶜBut the wrath has come upon them until the end.

This passage is a unity, though clearly it continues the thanksgiving of 1:2–10. Paul returns to the description of the congregation and reiterates the theme of 1:6 that the Thessalonians have remained steadfast in the word.

But now the horizon is widening. Whereas in 1:8 Paul spoke of Macedonia, Achaia and the whole mission field to herald the spread of the news of the Thessalonians' faith, here he expands the scope of the mission to the universal community consisting of both Jews and Gentiles.

2:13 The expression "the word of God that you heard from us"[99] stems from a blending of "word of God"[100] and "word of preaching."[101] Paul thus insists that his preaching *is* the word of God and that hearers encounter the word of God in his preaching.[102] He thanks God constantly, he says, because he knows that the Thessalonians have accepted the gospel he preached as the word of God.

2:14 The Thessalonian Christians' acceptance of God's word has triggered hostility among their own compatriots, with the result that they are in the same situation as the Christians in Judea, who have similarly suffered at the hands of their fellow-Jews.[103]

2:15–16 Paul expands on this last assertion by inserting an explanatory note that draws on traditions known in pre-Pauline communities. Here is a list of concurrences.

TRADITIONS IN I THESSALONIANS 2:15–16

1. The accusation that the Jews killed Jesus, which stands at the top of the charges, appears in the passion narratives[104] of the four gospels. Though the gospels were written between ten to forty years after Paul, they derive from very early traditions, according to which the Jewish authorities initiate proceedings against Jesus, condemn him to death, and hand him over to the Romans for execution.[105] So also, speeches by Peter and Stephen in Acts accuse the Jews of Jesus' murder.[106]

2:16 *Come upon/ahead of* 4:15.

2. The charge that the Jews killed the prophets[107] corresponds to the Old Testament theme of animosity toward prophetic opposition, a scheme that owes more to theological interpretation than to history. Jews had long ago formulated this charge against themselves, adding that Israel has been disobedient to God throughout its entire history.[108]

> [Elijah said to the Lord:] The people of Israel have forsaken your covenant, thrown down your altar and slain your *prophets* with the sword. (1 Kgs 19:10; cf. Rom 11:3)

> Nevertheless they were disobedient and rebelled against you and cast your law behind their back and killed your *prophets*, who had warned them in order to turn them back to you, and they committed great blasphemies. (Neh 9:26)

> [15]The Lord, the God of their fathers, sent them one messenger after another, hoping to spare his people and his dwelling place; [16]but they kept mocking the messengers of God, despising his words, and scoffing at the *prophets*, until the wrath of the Lord rose against his people and there was no remedy. (2 Chron 36:15–16)

> [20]For you have sent your anger and your wrath upon us, as you declared by your servants the *prophets*, saying: [21]Thus says the Lord: Bend your shoulders and serve the king of Babylon, and you will remain in the land that I gave to your ancestors. [22]But if you will not obey the voice of the Lord and will not serve the king of Babylon, [23]I will make to cease from the towns of Judah and from the region around Jerusalem the voice of mirth and the voice of gladness, the voice of the bridegroom and the voice of the bride, and the whole land will be a desolation without inhabitants.

> [24]But we did not obey your voice, to serve the king of Babylon; and you have carried out your threats, which you spoke by your servants the *prophets*, that the bones of our kings and the bones of our ancestors would be brought out of their resting-place; [25]and indeed they have been thrown out to the heat of day and the frost of night. They perished in great misery, by famine and sword and pestilence. [26]And the house that is called by your name you have made as it is today, because of the wickedness of the house of Israel. (Bar 2:20–26 NRSV [emphasis added])

3. Early Christian prophets edited these traditional charges, put them into Jesus' mouth and directed them against their own fellow Jews.[109]

> [11]Blessed are you when people revile you and persecute you and utter all kinds of evil against you falsely for my sake. [12]Rejoice and be jubilant, for your reward will be great in heaven. For so did they persecute the *prophets* before you. (Matt 5:11–12)

[29]Woe to you, scribes and Pharisees, you hypocrites! For you build tombs for *prophets* and adorn the graves of the righteous, [30]and say, If we had lived in the days of our fathers, we would not have taken part with them in shedding the blood of the *prophets*. [31]Thus you witness against yourselves that you are sons of those who murdered the *prophets*. [32]Fill up, then, the measure of your fathers. [33]You serpents, you brood of vipers! How are you to escape being sentenced to hell?

[34]Therefore, look, I send you *prophets*, sages, and scribes; and (some) of them you will kill and crucify, and (some) you will scourge in your synagogues and persecute from town to town. (Matt 23:29–34)

Jerusalem, Jerusalem, who kills the *prophets* and stones those who are sent to you! (Luke 13:34/Matt 23:37)

[47]Woe to you! For you build the tombs of the *prophets*, but your fathers killed them. [48]So you are witnesses and consent to the works of your fathers; for they killed them, and you build their tombs.

[49]Therefore also the Wisdom of God said, I will send them *prophets* and apostles, and (some) of them they will kill and persecute. (Luke 11:47–49)

4. Verse 15a–b has a parallel in the parable of the wicked tenants (Mark 12:1b–9), a traditional section that Mark has included almost verbatim in his gospel.[110] Note the correspondence between vital elements of the two:[111]

the killing of the prophets (1 Thess 2:15b/Mark 12:1b–5)
the killing of Jesus (1 Thess 2:15a/Mark 12:8)
the hindering of the mission (1 Thess 2:16/Mark 12:7, implied)
the prediction of a judgment of wrath against the Jews in 1 Thess 2:16c
     and the parabolic prediction in Mark 12:9 that the high priests,
     scribes, and elders[112] will be destroyed

5. The statement in v. 15 that the Jews do not please[113] God and oppose all people can be found in previous polemics of pagan authors against the Jews. For example, in the fifth book of his *Histories*, the Roman historian Tacitus (ca. 55–120 CE) composed an excursus on the Jews that Hans Conzelmann called the "most important text on ancient anti-Semitism, because of the material it contains and because of the personal and political evaluations made by the author, who looks back on the Jewish War [66–70 CE]. . . . This excursus summarizes practically everything that previous authors had said"[114] and mentions two peculiar ways of behavior among the Jews: *asebeia* (impiety or godlessness) and *misanthrôpia* (hostile refusal to have dealings with other people).[115]

Tacitus writes that the Jews of his time have become increasingly powerful and rigidly insist upon loyalty and faith . . . , whereas they adopt a spiteful and hostile attitude to all non-Jews. Those who go over to their religion observe the same customs, and the first thing to be inculcated upon them is the precept to despise the gods, to deny their fatherland and their parents and to regard their children and kinsfolk as worthless things. (*Histories* 5.5.1–2)

In the following I deal with only a few other writings and refer the reader to the detailed research on ancient anti-Semitism carried out by Conzelmann and Schäfer.[116]

At about the same time as Tacitus, the Jewish historian and apologist Josephus (around 40–110 CE) relates that the famous orator and grammarian Apollonius Molon (second to first century BCE)[117]

insults us (Jews) as atheists and misanthropes, and then blames us for fearfulness, and elsewhere charges us of rashness and reck-lessness. He says we are also the most untalented of barbarians. (*Against Apion* 2.148)

Similar statements are made by the Egyptian priest Manetho (third cen-tury BCE) and earlier by Hecateios of Abdera[118] who lived until 283/282 BCE.

In the Greek translation and continuation of the Old Testament book of Esther (first century BCE),[119] the Persian king Artaxerxes follows the advice of his councilor Haman to issue an order that all Jews, with their wives and children, who live in the Persian Empire be murdered. The primary reasons Haman offers are the Jews' fundamental resistance to political authority and their universal hostility to other human beings.

[4]Among all the nations in the world there is scattered a certain hostile people, who have laws contrary to those of every nation and continually disregard the ordinances of the kings. . . . [5]We under-stand that this people, and it alone, stands constantly in opposition to all human beings, perversely following a strange manner of life and laws, and is ill-disposed to our government, doing all the harm they can so that our kingdom may not attain stability. (Esth 13:4–5 RSV)

TRADITION AND REDACTION IN I THESSALONIANS 2:15–16

2:15 Paul's accusation that the Jews "persecuted us severely" in v. 15c is likely to derive from a tradition formulated by Greek-speaking Christian Jews who suffered harsh attacks from "non-Christian" Jews. One recalls that Paul him-self had persecuted such Christian Jews[120] before they introduced him to the Christian faith. It is therefore ironic "that it is precisely Paul, the former perse-cutor of Christians, who takes up a tradition which at one time applied to him and which he now uses against his former colleagues."[121]

Paul identifies himself with "us" in the tradition because as a Christian he had himself experienced persecution from the Jews[122] and—as he writes in 2 Cor 11:24—five times received from them the forty lashes minus one.[123] This is clearly an ecclesiastical "we"; it reflects Paul's persuasion that like Greek-speaking Christian Jews who had been persecuted by traditional Jews, he belongs to Christ because of their shared persecution.

2:16 As to the phrase "to fill up the measure" (v. 16b), note the Psalmist's metaphor of drinking a cup filled either with punishment or blessing[124] and Matt 23:32: "Fill up, then, the measure of your ancestors!"

In Paul's eyes the Jews had earned the cup of punishment by obstructing the spread of the gospel among the Gentiles (v. 16a). "Jewish opposition to his Gentile mission is nothing less than opposition to what God wills for humankind."[125] The assertion that God's wrath has come upon them (v. 16c) is Paul's reminder of the judgment (cf. 1:10). It may reflect an understanding of prophetic judgment that envisions a future act already beginning to happen in the present.[126]

In the Testament of Levi—which is usually dated in the second century BCE—we come across an announcement similar to that in v. 16. The text of TestLev 6:1 reads:

> But the wrath of God has come upon them unto the end.[127]

Either this text was interpolated into 1 Thess 2:16 or Paul and the author of the Testament of Levi used "a standard Jewish formula for declaring God's judgment."[128]

Be that as it may, Paul in 1 Thess 2:16 is clearly employing a tradition that his problems with non-Christian Jews would naturally have inclined him to adopt; and his personal experience is reflected in the added comment in v. 16a: "preventing us from speaking to the Gentiles that they may be saved." This thesis is based on the observation that five accusations against the Jews are connected by "and," while Paul adds his own interpretation without a conjunction.

In the original Greek of 1 Thess 2:14–16 all the accusations employ participial constructions,[129] a form which along with non-Pauline language strongly suggests tradition, and we find typically Pauline language in his comment at v. 16a.[130] On this last point it is worth noting that a number of similar expansions on traditions appear elsewhere in the Pauline letters without the apostle's specifically noting them.[131]

Thus Paul has purposefully adopted and deployed traditional polemic and included the coarse attack against the Jews in his letter, even if it was there before him in tradition. "As Paul does not indicate any reservations about this text we must assume that he adopts it because he shares its intentions."[132]

The Thessalonian Christians were surely aware of the Gentile accusation that the Jews are godless and hate all other nations on this earth.[133] Unique in this assault is that a Jew was employing Pagan anti-Jewish propaganda to incite

Gentile Christians against his fellow Jews. It can hardly be called an intra-Jewish attack,[134] and I am unable to think of another case of a self-described, committed Jew employing anti-Jewish polemic of pagan origin against his fellow Jews. I fail to see that "Paul's statements against the Jews (1 Thess. 2:14–16) are less intense than those in other places against Christian opponents (2 Cor. 11 or Gal. 2–5)."[135] Rather the virulent mixture of polemics that stems from both Jewish and Gentile backgrounds make the polemic in New Testament texts look pale by comparison.[136]

Thus the direction of the text of vv. 15–16 is plain: the unbelieving Jews who have earlier persecuted fellow Greek-speaking Christian Jews, and are now preventing Paul from preaching salvation to the Gentiles, have already incurred God's wrathful judgment. Five traditional attacks culminate in the sixth charge. Hence also the other charges are justified.

Paul's view of the church made up of Jews and Gentiles, a concept inherited from the community of Damascus that he persecuted,[137] is the positive analog of the negative verdict on Jewish disbelief. The Gentile Christians from Thessalonica, like the Christian communities of Judea and beyond, are members of a fellowship that is one in suffering and in Christ. "The association of the suffering of the Thessalonians with that of the Judaean churches served to build solidarity between Paul and his church at Thessalonica."[138] At the beginning of this letter, Paul had reminded the members of his Gentile Christian community of their election (1:4), a promise that equally applies to the churches in Judea.

I THESSALONIANS 2:17–3:8
Paul Longs to See the Thessalonians
The Sending and Return of Timothy

[17]But we, brothers, at the time in question orphaned from you in person, though not in heart, endeavored the more eagerly and with great desire to see you face to face. [18]For we wanted to come to you—I, Paul, again and again—but Satan hindered us.

[19]Who, then, is

> our hope
> or joy
> or crown of boasting

except for you before our Lord Jesus at his coming? [20]You are our glory and joy.

[3:1]Therefore when we could endure it no longer, we resolved to be left behind at Athens alone. [2]And we sent Timothy, our brother and God's fellow-

2:17 *See you face to face* 3:10.
2:19 *(Second) coming* 3:13; 4:15; 5:23.
3:1 *When we/I could endure it no longer* 3:5.

worker in the gospel of Christ, to strengthen and to comfort you in your faith, [3a]so that no one be shaken by these afflictions.

[3b]You yourselves know that we are destined for this. [4]For when we were with you, we told you beforehand that we were to suffer affliction; and as you know, it has come to pass.

[5]Therefore, when I could endure it no longer, I sent [Timothy] that I might learn of your faith, for fear that somehow the tempter had tempted you and that our labor had been in vain.

[6]But now Timothy has come to us from you, and has brought us the good news of your faith and love and reported that you always remember us kindly and long to see us, as we long to see you. [7]Therefore, we have been comforted, brothers, because of you in all our distress and affliction through your faith. [8]For now we live, if you stand firm in the Lord.

In 2:1–2 Paul wrote of his reception in Thessalonica and described in 2:13 how the Thessalonians had accepted the word preached by him as God's word. After the digression in 2:15–16 Paul turns to a report of events since his founding visit in Thessalonica. Two parentheses interrupt the account: 2:19–20 and 3:3b–4.

2:17–18 Repeating the address "brothers" from v. 14, Paul tells of a great desire to return to Thessalonica in person, and in v. 18 employs an emphatic "I, Paul" to assert the strength of his motivation.[139] The explanation he offers for not coming[140] is that Satan prevented his travel. The real reason for not returning to Thessalonica remains unknown.

2:19–20 This section interrupts the description of Paul's thwarted travel plans, but the topic will soon be picked up in 3:1. In v. 19 Paul alludes to the end-time perspective of Christian life in claiming that the Thessalonian community constitutes his hope of salvation at the second coming of Jesus, when both he and they can rely on receiving deliverance.[141] This, Paul intimates by the question "Who then is our hope . . . but you?" and in a fine rhetorical flourish answers his own question in v. 20: "You are our glory and joy."

3:1–3a In v. 1 Paul returns to the report begun in 2:17–18. Satan having kept him from visiting the congregation, he sent his co-worker Timothy from Athens[142] to strengthen and to comfort the Thessalonians not to be discouraged by the afflictions that resulted from their having accepted Paul's message (1:6). He understands their troubles as "the historical frame within which the acceptance of the word occurs."[143] Passages from 1 Corinthians illuminate this:

The distress (is) impending. (1 Cor 7:26)
The appointed time has grown very short. (1 Cor 7:29)
The form of this world is passing away. (1 Cor 7:31)

3:3b–4 Like 2:19 this is a parenthesis. In the epistolary context it repeats Timothy's message: do not be moved by these trials, but rather understand the present time of troubles as part of a triumphal destiny.

3:5 This picks up vv. 1–2; the connecting phrase is "when I (we) could not endure it any longer."

3:6 In telling of Timothy's return and good news, Paul uses the nouns "faith" and "love" to describe the spiritual health of the Thessalonians, and the verb "to remember" to evoke the optimistic beginning of the letter (1:3)—though here, of course, it is the community remembering the apostle. But in either case Paul stresses the unity of apostle and community.

3:7–8 Paul is encouraged by the good news from Thessalonica, and once again the roles are reversed; for whereas in v. 2 the apostle sent Timothy to comfort the Thessalonians, now they ease his worries. Community and apostle share distress and affliction and provide mutual encouragement.

I THESSALONIANS 3:9–13
Thanksgiving and Prayer

[9]How can we thank God enough for you, for all the joy in which we rejoice before God for your sake? [10]We pray earnestly night and day that we may see you face to face and complete whatever may be lacking in your faith.

[11]Now may our God and Father, and our Lord Jesus, direct our way to you.

[12]And may the Lord make you increase and excel more and more in love to one another and to all, as we do to you—[13a]in order to strengthen your hearts without blame in Sanctity before our God and Father, [13b]at the coming of our Lord Jesus with all his saints.

3:9 Beginning anew, as it were, Paul now completes the great thanksgiving. By means of a rhetorical question he derives new meaning "from the experience with the community with respect to the thanks which of course are due to God."[144]

3:10 Paul's entreaty to greet the Thessalonians in person reiterates the wish in v. 6, where we also read that the Thessalonians longed for Paul's presence. Once again we find the theme of reciprocity between apostle and community. Paul's goal of completing whatever may be lacking in their faith seems a bit puzzling, since in v. 8 he had invoked the firmness of the Thessalonians' faith. Perhaps it was a lack of spiritual presence that he sensed and hoped they also felt. Or perhaps it is a veiled reference to the apparent anxiety of the community caused by the recent deaths of several members—an uneasiness that he attempts to neutralize in 4:13–17.

3:11–13 This section is a transition, for the prayer in v. 11 that Paul may once again visit the Thessalonians advances the train of thought and the request that God strengthen the internal bonds of the community introduces the next section.[145]

3:12 *Excel more and more* 4:1, 10.
3:13 *Sanctity, saints, sanctification* 4:3–4. 7; 5:26.

We see in v. 13 that the topic of Jesus' second coming remains important, a theme that becomes a vital concern in 4:13–5:11. The noun "sanctity" (v. 13a) introduces the theme that will be central to the next section (4:1–4:12), and thus prepares the reader for Paul's exhortation that the members of the community attain sanctity.

The expression "with all his saints" refers to Jesus' coming not with the resurrected Christians[146] but rather with the angels.[147]

I THESSALONIANS 4:1–12
Sanctification of the Members of the Community

⁴˙¹Finally, brothers, we ask and exhort you in the Lord Jesus that just as you received from us how to live and please God, as indeed you are living, so may you excel more and more. ²For you know what instructions we gave you through the Lord Jesus Christ.

³This, then, is the will of God and your sanctification:

that you abstain from fornication;

⁴that each of you take for himself a vessel (wife) in sanctification and honor, ⁵not in the passion of lust like the Gentiles who do not know God;

⁶ᵃthat nobody wrong or exploit his brother in your dealings with him.

⁶ᵇFor the Lord is an avenger in all these things—
⁶ᶜas indeed we have predicted and solemnly affirmed.
⁷For God has not called us to uncleanness but to sanctification.
⁸Therefore whoever disregards this, disregards not people but God, who gives his Holy Spirit to you.

⁹But concerning brotherly love, you do not need to have anyone write to you, for you yourselves have been taught by God to love one another ¹⁰and indeed you do (love) all the brothers throughout Macedonia.

But we urge you, brothers, to excel more and more,

¹¹to aspire to live quietly,
to mind your own affairs, and
to work with your own hands—as we charged you—

¹²so that you behave properly toward outsiders, and become dependent on nobody.

Verses 1–3a and v. 8 frame the first part of this section, in which Paul develops his founding proclamation by dealing with the topic of sanctification. Vv. 9–12 resemble a catechism.[148]

The content is thoroughly Jewish. The Gentile-Christian Thessalonians are not to live like other Gentiles (v. 5), but must behave as if they were Jews.[149] Indeed, as v. 6b–8 show, veneration of the one God of the Jewish scriptures is to undergird their way of life.

The syntax of the original Greek in v. 1 is rough. Paul meant to say, "We ask and urge you in the Lord Jesus Christ to continue your progress in living as we taught you and thus to please God." But it seems that as he was dictating the letter he decided to insert a compliment to the community ("as you are now doing") and thus garbled the sentence construction. The above translation attempts to clarify his meaning.

4:3a admonishes the Thessalonians to sanctify themselves by fulfilling God's will, and serves as the topic sentence of vv. 3b–6.

4:3b The infinitive construction in vv. 3b–6a, which cannot be reproduced in the translation, defines sanctification: a) abstinence from fornication, b) avoidance of lustful passion, and c) treating others with fairness and respect.

4:4a–5 Paul exhorts husbands "to restrict their sexual activity to their own wives and to enter on this with them in sanctification and honor."[150] "Vessel" is a metaphor for one's wife, into which the husband puts his semen.[151] To avoid *porneia* one must take only one's wife as a sexual other half. This "is consistent with 1 Cor 7:2, where Paul directs that 'because of cases of sexual immorality (*porneia*) each man should have his own wife and each woman her own husband.'"[152] The Jewish tradition adopted by Paul constantly accused "Gentiles" of non-marital sexuality and called this "sexual immorality" or "fornication." Indeed, in Paul's catalogues of vice, "fornication" usually stands at the top of the list.[153] Paul demands that the Thessalonians practice marriage in sanctification and honor rather than give way to lust as Gentiles do (v. 5a).

4:6a The demand to be honest in dealing with one's Christian brother is the focus of the final exhortation. Paul tells the Thessalonians not to "wrong"[154] or to "exploit"[155] one's brother. What Paul understands to mean by "to wrong" he explains thus: "not to exploit the brother in your dealings with him.[156] Locating this command here suggests that in Paul's mind greediness[157] and fornication belong together.[158] Paul depends here on Jewish ethics.[159]

4:6b–c The threat in v. 6b recalls an Old Testament psalm,[160] and warns that God will punish all those who do not perform his will and who do not follow the commands and prohibitions listed in v. 3b–6a. In v. 6c Paul reminds his listeners that during his first visit he had instructed them about the punitive side of God.

4:7 The catchword "sanctification" provides a connection to v. 3 and "emphasizes the mandatory character of sanctification . . . that derives from God's action of calling."[161] "Uncleanness"[162] was used earlier in the letter (2:3) in a list of three vices ("fraud, uncleanness, deceit") and is now employed by Paul as opposed to sanctification.[163]

4:8 Paul again underlines the necessity of fulfilling God's will. Whoever rejects God's call to sanctification thereby rejects God,[164] the giver of the Spirit. "The reception of the Spirit is connected with baptism and then remains a permanent gift."[165]

4:9–10 Paul turns to the topic of brotherly love, specifically the spiritual bond that exists between fellow-Christians. As he does later in 5:1, Paul employs the rhetorical ploy of *paraleipsis* by denying the necessity of mentioning something (in this case, brotherly love) that he then expands upon. Concerning this virtue, the apostle describes the Thessalonians as having been "taught by God," a phrase that in Old Testament prophecies indicates salvation.[166] Paul assures the Thessalonians that they have demonstrated brotherly love toward both one another and their fellow believers throughout Macedonia.

4:11–12 In v. 11 Paul reminds the community of three demands comprising brotherly love that he had transmitted to them in his inaugural preaching, and he now calls on them to aspire to achieve these demands ever more fully: a) to live quietly, b) to mind one's own affairs, and c) to take care of one's own needs ("work with your own hands").

These precepts are widely found among popular philosophers,[167] but have no specific relation to the new faith.[168] Indeed Paul has rather loosely attached them to the preceding section. The term "properly" (v. 12)[169] summarizes Paul's message; in Hellenistic ethical teaching it epitomizes moral rectitude.[170] Besides, the virtues here enumerated match the ethics of Hellenistic Judaism derived from the Greek Old Testament (LXX) under the influence of contemporary philosophy:

> Worshipping one God (1 Thess 1:9/Exod 20:2)
> Turning away from idols (1 Thess 1:9/Exod 20:3–4)
> Avoiding fornication (1 Thess 4:3/Exod 20:13/Tob 4:12)
> Avoiding fraud (1 Thess 4:6/Exod 20:16–17/Lev 19:13)
> Loving one's brother and one another (1 Thess 4:9/Lev 19:18)

Note that for Paul sanctification involved not only following certain commandments, but also separation from all things that would defile, especially from within the congregation.[171] The reason for this lies in the sanctity of the community that constitutes "the temple of God,"[172] and thus corresponds to the holiness of God.[173]

Arthur Darby Nock derived from stylistic similarities between Paul's epistles and the diatribe—a contemporary "type of philosophical causerie"—the proposal that Paul adopted both the form and content of Cynic philosophers he had heard engaged in public debate.[174] "Cynic philosophers talked at street corners to any and all who would listen, and Paul must have heard them at times; and much of what they said was reasonably congenial, for the Cynics attacked popular vices, and popular superstitions."[175]

Equally striking is the fact that there is not a paragraph in Paul's writing that does not suggest subliminal recollections of the Greek Bible. Indeed, as Nock himself observes, Paul "shows only the slightest acquaintance with pagan Greek literature, but he knew his Old Testament very well."[176]

I THESSALONIANS 4:13–18
The Fate of the Deceased Christians[177]

[13]But we do not want you to be ignorant, brothers, concerning those who are asleep, so that you may not grieve like the rest who have no hope.
[14]For since we believe that

> Jesus died and rose,

so also God through Jesus will bring with him those who have fallen asleep.
[15a]For this we say to you by a word of the Lord,

[15b]that we who are alive, who are left until the Lord's coming,
shall by no means precede those who have fallen asleep.

[16]For the Lord himself will descend from heaven
> with a cry of command,
> with the archangel's call,
> with the sound of the trumpet of God.
And the dead in Christ will rise first;
> [17]then we who are alive, who are left,
> shall be caught up in the clouds together with them
> to meet the Lord in the air;
and so we shall forever be with the Lord.

[18]Therefore comfort each other with these words.

1 Thess 4:13–17 and 5:1–11 constitute a separate section of the epistle. The sudden change of subject is dramatic: Paul finds it necessary to respond to a question from Thessalonica concerning the fate of those who have fallen asleep—more specifically, those who have died before Jesus' promised return.

The parallel formulations in 4:18 and 5:11 ("Therefore comfort each other . . .") suggest that these matters are affecting the unity and morale of the community, a possibility that may be reflected in the placement of this section in the letter as a whole. For if this letter originated as an effort in "damage control" in the face of growing disaffection that arose when members of

---

4:13 Being/having fallen asleep 4:14–15. Like the rest 5:5.
4:14 Rise 4:16.
4:18 Comfort each other 5:11.

the community died before Jesus' promised imminent return, then Paul faced a problem of potentially devastating proportions. An answer must be given, but the urgency of the issue must be minimized. How better do that than to raise the issue late in the letter after repeated reassurances that all is well, to introduce and dispose of the matter in five verses certified by a direct communication from the Lord himself, and then, just before the closing verses, shift to a related topic that offers a good deal less threat and more reassurance, and then exhort folk to comfort one another with these thoughts.

For clearly 1 Thess 4:13–17 and 5:1–11 seek to assure the future union with Christ of both the dead and the living at Jesus' second coming; indeed, the verbs "to be awake" and "to sleep" in 5:10—by which Paul obviously intends to interpret "to live" and "to be dead"—underline the close relation between 5:1–11 and the problem of 4:13–18, namely the relationship of the dead to the living at the expected second coming.

STRUCTURE OF I THESSALONIANS 4:13–18

Introduction: Following the death of several Thessalonian Christians, Paul seeks to prevent the spread of a sense of disillusionment and blighted hopes that has apparently affected the community (v. 13).

First response to the problem: Assurance that Jesus' resurrection promises the union of the dead with the Lord at his second coming (v. 14).

Second response to the problem: Assurance in the form of a word of the Lord that at the time of Jesus' second coming the dead Christians will not be preceded by the living to meet the Lord in the air (vv. 15–17).

Content of the declaration (v. 15)

Description of the *parousia* and rapture (vv. 16–17).

Conclusion: Exhortation that members of the community share this message among themselves and thus find consolation and peace of mind (v. 18)

4:13–14 Paul often uses the introductory formula "we would not have you ignorant" (v. 13) to introduce something new or to present the congregation with previously unknown information.[178]

"Jesus died and rose" is a formula of faith that has many parallels in the New Testament and especially in the letters of Paul.[179] One wonders why Paul did not write "Jesus died and was raised." He probably did this to stress the parallelism between Jesus' rising and the rising of the dead, which is narrated in v. 16.[180]

The change of subjects in v. 14—*Jesus* died and rose (v. 14a); *God* will bring with him the dead (v. 14b)—is a stylistically clumsy construction that is singular among Paul's creedal formulations. The stylistic awkwardness is further increased by the phrase "through Jesus," which refers to "bring with him." The construction is awkward: God will bring the dead through Jesus with Jesus.

Since the preposition "through" (*dia*) indicates the means by which the union with Christ is achieved, I am inclined to assume that Paul had in mind the creedal formula "Jesus died for us." In the apostle's view, then, the purpose of Jesus' death was that through his sacrifice, God might unite Christians with him. (See 1 Thess 5:9–10 and the interpretive note.)

The syntax, however disjointed, still calls for an explanation. It can be adequately explained only on the assumption that Paul is for the first time connecting the confession of Jesus' death and resurrection with the death of Christians. When he does this, he maintains the old theological principle that had been proclaimed in Thessalonica and that conceived of Jesus' death and resurrection as a signal of his imminent return from heaven. The existence of this concept is evident from Paul's summary of his missionary proclamation in 1 Thess 1:9–10 (cf. 3:13).

Apparently the death of Christians was not a topic of this initial proclamation for the simple reason that the return of Jesus was thought to be immediately at hand. But in the first theological reflection on the death of a few Christians, salvation resulting from fellowship with the Lord at his return becomes highly important.

An indication that "hope" in 1 Thessalonians is not understood primarily as hope for the resurrection arises from a comparison of our passage with 1 Cor 6:14. There it is stated, "And God raised the Lord and will also raise us up by his power." A corresponding final statement for 1 Thess 4:14 would have been, "Thus God will also raise those who have fallen asleep." While 1 Cor 6:14 explicates the resurrection of Christians according to the schema "as Christ—so the Christians," this schema has no importance in 1 Thess 4:14. The statement about the resurrection of Christians is only indirectly important, for while their resurrection is the presupposition for being brought together with Christ, the emphasis is not placed on it.

I am grateful to have received support in this matter from Karl Paul Donfried:

> Lüdemann is correct in defining Paul's hope in this letter as a parousia-hope and not a resurrection-hope. Further, he is also to be followed when he urges that the introduction of the resurrection of the prematurely deceased Christians does not decisively alter Paul's earlier view that the union of Christians with Christ will be at the parousia. This new information functions to preserve the eschatological hope of the early Paul and it does not introduce a new doctrine of resurrection-hope. That only follows in 1 Corinthians.[181]

Thus Paul did not deal with the resurrection of Christians during the foundation-proclamation in Thessalonica. As the result of the incipient *delay of the parousia*, Paul introduces the auxiliary notion of the resurrection of the dead Christians. "The image of the resurrection has slipped in between."[182] The general resurrection of the dead and the judgment are not affected by this addition. This process would hardly be understandable twenty years after the death of Jesus, though not if this time were halved.

4:15–17 Paul begins v. 15 with "for" (in Greek, *gar*) because he understands these verses as further support for what he said in v. 14. "This we say to you" refers to the entire noun clause comprising v. 15b and marks the beginning of a new element in the argument.

Questions arise concerning the meaning of "by a word of the Lord."[183] Research has suggested two possibilities: a) It is based on a saying of the earthly Jesus. b) It stems from a reported saying of the "risen Lord" that derived either from a prophetic pronouncement or a visionary experience of Paul.

Further, the delimitation of the saying of the Lord is uncertain. While most interpreters find it to consist of vv. 16–17 and understand all of v. 15 as a Pauline summary of the saying and its application to the Thessalonian situation, some exegetes view v. 15b as the essence of the saying of the Lord and vv. 16–17 as narrative details.

THE DISPARITY OF 4:15 AND 4:16–17

Verse 15 is written in epistolary style, as is clear from the first person plural, whereas v. 16 is exclusively third person, and v. 17 is, like v. 15b, exclusively first plural. Verse 15 is clearly intended to reassure the Thessalonians concerning a specific issue, whereas vv. 16–17 offer a general description of events at the end of time.

As is clear from the statement that the living shall not precede the dead, v. 15b is speaking of a moment of time *after* the events pictured in v. 16 and contemporaneous with those described in v. 17. The reassurance in v. 15 evidently finds the primary importance of vv. 16–17 concentrated in the statement about being caught up in the clouds (v. 17.) It is hardly a coincidence that the clause "we who are alive, who are left" (v. 15b) is repeated in v. 17.

Observation of these tensions in vv. 15–17 permits us to make the preliminary suggestion that v. 15 and vv. 16–17 do not belong to the same layer of tradition. Rather v. 15 offers an advance exegesis of vv. 16–17.

THE "WORD OF THE LORD" IN I THESSALONIANS 4:15

Previous research has focused primarily on the question of whether this verse predicates the earthly Jesus or the risen Christ.

For one thing, the gospels contain no real parallel to the verse's content.[184] For another, designating such a saying as an unwritten word (*agraphon*) is always a precarious undertaking.[185] This is especially the case with this saying, since the relationship of the *kyrios* in the saying to the *kyrios* who supposedly uttered it is unclear. Accordingly, this *logos kyriou* should be understood as a saying of the risen Christ reported by a prophet or apostle in the name of the *kyrios*, who supposedly spoke it.[186] That is to say, Paul understands this as a saying of the risen one, but the kernel of vv. 16–17 derives from a Jewish apocalyptic text, which Paul took to be a saying of the Lord.[187]

An analogy from the beginnings of Christianity for such a process of placing a Jewish apocalyptic text onto the lips of the "risen" Jesus one is found in Mark 13, where a Jewish apocalyptic text clearly shines through as the kernel (13:7–8, 12, 14–22, 24–27) of the apocalyptic speech. "Important . . . [is] the fact that a Jewish apocalypse was taken over and used as a saying of Jesus, so that the Messiah (21f.) or the Son of Man (26f.) was simply identified with Jesus."[188]

THE MEANING OF I THESSALONIANS 4:16–17 AT THE LEVEL OF THE PAULINE REDACTION

Here we must attempt to determine not only Paul's understanding of the passage, but finally the meaning of the Pauline additions to the Jewish substratum. The former need naturally arises from the mere adoption of the Jewish substratum and its particular statements for the situation of the Thessalonian congregation.

The separation of redaction and tradition reveals the following Pauline additions:[189] "(dead) in Christ," "first/then," "we who are alive," "together with them," "and so we shall always be with the Lord." Further, Paul has changed the third person—that in the presentation of the substratum referred to the dead and to the survivors—into the first person. Finally, Paul seems to have modified the traditional order, "*parousia* . . . resurrection," so that the resurrection has been inserted between the beginning of the *parousia* and its completion. The Pauline redaction of the substratum and the interest expressed through the mere adoption of this substratum reveal two concerns: the problem of the fate of Christians who die before the *parousia*—an issue that has arisen because of the death of several members of the Thessalonian community—and a desire to emphasize the expectation of the *parousia*.

Paul is able to employ the Jewish substratum because it speaks of the imminence of these final events. He radicalizes and actualizes the statement that a "remnant"—designated by the verb *perileipomai*—will be raised to join the Lord in the clouds by adding to it the imminent expectation he had nurtured at the time of his founding of the community.[190] The specification "We who are alive, who are left" strongly implies that either Paul does not expect further deaths or that the *parousia* will come in his lifetime and that of most of the Thessalonian faithful.

At the level of the Pauline redaction, the "dead" in the tradition become the "dead in Christ." The meaning of the text is adequately expressed by observing that the addition "in Christ" indicates merely that those who have died were Christians. It must also be taken into account that when 1 Thessalonians was written, the issue of the future of dead Christians had not yet been theologically mastered.

The precise meaning of "in Christ" after "dead" involves both a recognition that "in Christ" has a technical meaning and also that Paul uses the qualification "in Christ" to indicate that death cannot hinder future fellowship with Christ.[191] Such a loss of fellowship and its attendant assurances was evidently the fear that arose in Thessalonica after the first deaths occurred. Paul's answer: Those "in Christ" will always be "with Christ," a status that in turn is founded on the powerful commitment of faith that admits one to the special relationship of being "in Christ."

A similar observation can be made regarding v. 14, where Paul employed "through Jesus" to indicate expressly that the "saving event" of the death and resurrection of Jesus described in the creed (v. 14)[192] was the *reason* that the dead would continue to participate in fellowship with Christ.

Thus Paul's statement in v. 15b, just as in vv. 16–17, points in two directions. It takes a stand on the fate of the dead and it insists on the imminence of the expected return of the Lord Jesus.

One element of the statement in v. 15b is an assurance that those who have died will not be preceded to their eternal reward by those still alive at the *parousia*. The wording of this statement reminds one of the concerns expressed in the Jewish apocalypses for the fate of the dead (see further below). With regard to the Thessalonian situation, this statement can be correctly understood only by recalling that the goal of Christian hope is fellowship with the Lord at the end of time. This goal is reflected

at the end of v. 14 ("God will bring with him")
at the end of v. 17 ("We shall always be with the Lord")
in v. 15 ("until the Lord's coming")

"We who are alive, we who are left" is also found in v. 17; in fact, it has been taken over from there. One should notice how the imminent expectation is radicalized. "The present passive participle in 4.15b, *perileipomenoi*, indicates that the entire drama has begun and is being worked out now."[193] In his redaction, Paul equates the "remnant" in the tradition with the surviving majority in the present case; more than that, he has transcended the notion of the remnant by his assurance in v. 15 that all Christians still alive will survive until the *parousia*.

Thus the two aims of the Pauline statements in v. 15b and vv. 16–17 prove to be identical in form and content. One final point should be noted: the emphatic reassurance in v. 15 that the living will not precede the dead presupposes that some had questioned whether the Christians who had died would be united with Christ at all. But this problem indicates that in his initial preaching Paul had not dealt with the fate of Christians who might die before Jesus' return—that is, with the nature of Christian resurrection.

RESULT

The death of some members of the congregation in Thessalonica had led others in the congregation into a grief or doubt comparable only with the hopelessness of the heathen. The death of a few fellow Christians had threatened the hope and expectation (*elpis*) of the congregation that, via the notion of the *parousia*, was directed towards future fellowship with Christ. The question that arose was "Will the dead miss out on future fellowship with Christ?" By invoking and applying the delivered message of faith, the traditional credo of the death and resurrection of Christ, Paul offers assurance that Christians who die prior to the *parousia* will participate in the future fellowship (v. 14).

In the second part of the section, Paul provides further confirmation for this thesis—which was clearly *new* to the Thessalonians. He does this by adducing a "word of the Lord" that he derived from a Jewish apocalyptic text and accommodates to the situation by editorial additions. This saying elucidates Paul's own assumption that the Christian dead will rise. When the *parousia* arrives, they will suffer absolutely no disadvantage, but rather will be raised at the beginning of the end and thus enjoy the same situation as the living, whereupon both groups will participate in full fellowship with Christ.

This statement does not imply that Paul rejected the idea of a general resurrection—he was, of course, a Pharisee, and he acknowledged the resurrection of Jesus—but it does indicate that he believed Jesus' second coming and the end of the age to be imminent. None of this is intended to deny that the doctrine of a general resurrection could have been part of Paul's initial proclamation at Thessalonica. One should, however, differentiate from this issue the question of how Paul presented the future hope that was available to him and his congregation.

My conclusion is that the unanticipated delay in Jesus' second coming has required Paul to introduce the complementary notion of the resurrection of the dead in Christ (*hoi nekroi en Christō*)[194] in order to maintain the Old Testament conception of God's favored ones being lifted up into heaven.[195] This inclusion of those who had recently died would not deny the doctrine of general resurrection of the dead and the final judgment, for it would not affect these concepts—though to be sure, fewer and fewer would find such a forecast believable as the years went on.

THE JEWISH BACKGROUND OF I THESSALONIANS 4:16–17[196]

The report of the appearance of the Son of Man in 4 Ezra 13 is particularly similar to our passage:

> [3]I looked, and behold, this wind made something like the figure of a man come up out of the heart of the sea. And I looked, and behold, that man flew with the clouds of heaven; . . . [4]and whenever his voice issued from his mouth, all who heard his voice melted as

wax melts when it feels the fire. . . . [12]After this I saw the same
man come down from the mountain. . . . [13]Then many people came
to him. . . . [48]Those who are left of your people . . . shall be saved.
(4 Ezra 13:3–13, 48[197])

It is well known that 4 Ezra does not connect the messianic kingdom with the
resurrection of the dead. According to Pseudo-Ezra, "those who are left are
more blessed than those who have died" (13:24). The resurrection of the dead
will occur only after the messianic reign has drawn to an end:

> [32]The earth shall give up those who are asleep in it, and the dust
> those who dwell silently in it, and the chambers shall give up the
> souls which have been committed to them. [33]And the Most High
> shall be revealed upon the seat of judgment. (4 Ezra 7:32–33[198])

However, the separation of the intervening messianic kingdom from the future eon and the concurrent resurrection of the dead reflect a conception that
can be documented only for the period after 70 CE. Prior to that time Jewish
belief in the resurrection is closely connected with the coming time of salvation, which is identical with the messianic kingdom. "Thus the Old Testament
passage Daniel 12:2 [is] the only one other than Isaiah 26:19 [that] seeks to
answer the question of whether the pious ones who do not live to experience
the change of worlds at the initiation of the blessed era will miss out on salvation. The answer is supplied precisely by the belief in the resurrection."[199]

A question that calls for further clarification pertains to the relationship of
those who are lifted up while yet alive to those who are raised from the dead.
Do Jewish apocalyptic texts deal with the relationship of these two groups, or
must we have recourse to the thesis that the fragmentary nature of the apocalypse contained in vv. 16–17 makes its derivation from tradition impossible?

Almost all apocalypses share the conviction that the end is at hand. Even
the first apocalyptic teacher "is convinced that he will experience the end
of times; this conviction is maintained throughout the ages."[200] Since these
writers expected the resurrection of the dead to be part of the imminent era of
salvation, one should expect to find somewhere reflections on the relationship
of the survivors to those who are raised. Consider the so-called Apocalypse of
Baruch written in the late first or early second century CE:

> [30:1] . . . When the time of the appearance of the Anointed One has
> been fulfilled and he returns with glory, then all who sleep in hope
> of him will rise. [2] . . . And it will happen at that time that those
> treasuries will be opened in which the number of the souls of the
> righteous were kept, and they will go out and the multitudes of the
> souls will appear together, in one assemblage, of one mind, and the
> first ones will enjoy themselves and the last ones will not be sad.

³For they know that the time has come of which it is said, that it is the end of times. (2 Bar 30:1–3[201])

Chapter 49 of Baruch seems to present chapters 29–30 in a varied form and to have arisen from apologetic interest. The apocalyptic inquires in 49:2, "In which shape will the living live in your day?" The Mighty One gives the following answer:

¹Listen, Baruch, to these words and write down in the memory of your heart all that you shall learn. ²For the earth shall surely give back the dead at that time; it receives them now in order to keep them, not changing anything in their form. But as it has received them it will give them back. . . . ³For then it will be necessary to show those who live the dead are living again, and that those who went away have come back. ⁴And it will be when they have recognized each other, those who know each other at this moment, then my judgment will be strong, and those things which have been spoken of before will come. (2 Bar 50:1–4[202])

Baruch is one example of how apocalyptic circles in Judaism viewed the relationship between the survivors and the dead at the time of salvation. The righteous, both those still alive and those who have died, will participate in the time of salvation, which is inaugurated by the arrival of the Messiah and the subsequent raising of the dead. Then both the survivors and those resurrected will be transformed after the judgment (50:8).

According to 4 Ezra the judgment of God takes place at one time and thus no group will enjoy chronological preference:

⁴¹I said, Yet look, O Lord, you have charge of those who are alive at the end, but what will those do who were before us, or we, or those who come after us? ⁴²He said to me, I shall liken my judgment to a circle; just as for those who are last there is now slowness, so for those who are first there is no haste. (4 Ezra 5:41–42[203])

Yet elsewhere the same writing expresses the idea that the living have an advantage over the deceased:

¹⁶Woe to those who will survive in those days. And still more, woe to those who do not survive. ¹⁷For those who do not survive will be sorrowful, ¹⁸because they understand what is in store for the last days, but not attaining it. ¹⁹But woe also to those who do survive, for this reason—they shall see great dangers and much distress, as these dreams show. ²⁰Yet it is better to come into these things, though incurring peril, than to pass from the world like a

cloud, and not to see what shall happen in the last days. (4 Ezra 13:16–20[204])

Since Paul is known to have been a student of past and contemporary Jewish literary traditions, and since those traditions can be assumed to have persisted at the time of Paul, it is entirely reasonable to propose that these texts provide a background against which to read 1 Thess 4:16–17.

1 THESSALONIANS 5:1–11
About the Coming of the Lord's Day

5:1But as to the times and dates, brothers, you do not no need to have anything written to you.

2For you yourselves know full well that the day of the Lord will come like a thief in the night. 3When people say, "There is peace and security," then sudden destruction will come upon them just as the pain of childbirth [comes] upon a pregnant woman, and they will not escape.

4But you, brothers, are not in such darkness that the day could come upon you like a thief;

5afor all of you are sons of light and sons of the day.

5bWe are not of the night or of darkness. 6So then let us not sleep like the rest, but let us keep awake and be sober.

7For those who sleep, sleep at night;

and those who get drunk, get drunk at night.

8But since we belong to the day, let us be sober, and put on the breastplate of faith and love, and as a helmet the hope for salvation.

9For God has not destined us for wrath, but to obtain salvation through our Lord Jesus Christ,

10who died for us

so that whether we wake or sleep we might live with him.

11Therefore comfort each other and build one another up, as indeed you do.

STRUCTURE OF 1 THESSALONIANS 5:1–11
Topic: Time and hour of the second coming (v. 1)
Proclamation of the incalculability of the Day of the Lord (vv. 2–3)
Statements of assurance (vv. 4–5)
Admonitions (vv. 6–8)
Christological argument related to 4:14, 17 (vv. 9–10)
Common consolation related to 4:18 (v. 11)

5:2 Day (of the Lord) 5:4–5, 8.
5:8 Salvation, save 5:9.

5:1 The preposition "about"[205] (here rendered "as to") is used for the third time[206] and again indicates a question by the Thessalonians. The phrase "times and dates" stems from prophetic claims about the nearness of the end.[207] As he did earlier, Paul here employs the rhetorical figure of *paraleipsis* by declaring unnecessary the reminder he includes.[208]

5:2 Why is it unnecessary to teach the Thessalonians about coming Day of the Lord? Because they know from the founding proclamation that it will come without warning and when least expected, like a thief at night.[209] Indeed, Paul likely presented much the same doctrine to each of his congregations at the time of the founding visit.[210]

5:3 The image of a pregnant woman[211] dramatically impresses on the listener or reader that the coming of the end is inevitable. The present verse "thus confirms that in 1:10 the future judgment of destruction is in view. Christians will be saved from it by Jesus in that they are lifted to heaven."[212]

The slogan "peace and security" reflects the political propaganda of the early imperial period; it was one element of a Roman creed with which the Thessalonian Christians were well acquainted. "In that Paul aims his eschatological preaching directly at the ideology of the Roman Empire, he makes it clear that the near coming of Jesus—as he conceives of it—signifies the destruction of the Roman Empire."[213] Until then, as Paul indicates in his letter to the Romans, Christians should submit to the ruling authorities, for they have been instituted by God.[214]

5:4 "Brothers" picks up the same noun from v. 1; "darkness" is related to "night" at v. 2 and "day" echoes "day of the Lord" at v. 2. On "thief" cf. also v. 2. Since the Thessalonian Christians are not in the darkness, the Day of the Lord cannot come upon them like a thief.

5:5a Rather, they are "sons of the light," employing a beatitude that may be an allusion to a baptismal formula.[215]

5:5b From here through v. 10 the apostle uses the first person plural, perhaps to reinforce the assertion of blessedness in v. 5a and to emphasize the apostolic assurance that the Christians in Thessalonica belong neither to the night nor to the darkness.

5:6 This verse picks up the phrase "not grieve like the rest" from 4:13; here, changing the imagery only slightly, he writes, "not sleep like the rest." "Not to sleep" and "to be awake" pick up the previous day and night imagery, and together with "to be sober" constitute Pauline descriptions of the Christian's preparation for the imminent end.[216]

5:7 In a parenthetic further expansion of this metaphoric exhortation, sleep and drunkenness are associated with night.

5:8 A shift in imagery reflects Isa 59:17 (LXX), which reads: "And he [the Lord] put on righteousness as a breast-plate, and placed the helmet of salvation on his head; and he clothed himself with the garment of vengeance."

The elements and sequence of Paul's triad—faith, love, hope—match those at 1:3. "The way Paul connects the triad with the breast-plate and the helmet gives special importance to the last part, namely hope. It has a major importance for the perseverance of Christian life."[217]

5:9–10 According to v. 9 Christians are not intended to suffer God's wrath, i.e., the destruction that 1:10 assigns to the Gentiles and 2:16 promises for the Jews. Rather, their salvation is ordained in advance.

The phrase "Jesus died for us/for our sins" is a short creedal formula that Paul had learned as a convert.[218] It expresses the atoning effect of Jesus' death and thus underwrites the Christian's future life, which commences with Jesus' second coming.

"JESUS DIED FOR US" AS A PRE-PAULINE CREEDAL FORMULA

The idea of Jesus' death as atonement for sins seems to come not from Jerusalem, but from Damascus.[219] The Jerusalem disciples, whose conceptualization of Christianity depended largely on the Hebrew Bible—in which vicarious atonement for another's guilt can hardly be found—was unlike that of Greek-speaking Jews, who were familiar with the idea of dying for the benefit of others. From the classical period onwards, Greeks recognized and admired voluntary death in the service of one's city or one's friends.[220] But in Hellenistic Judaism, it is only after the time of the Maccabean Revolt that we find the repeated theme of martyrs dying for the people or for the Law, and thereby atoning for the sins of others.[221]

Upon accepting the message that Jesus had been raised from the dead, therefore, Greek-speaking Jews interpreted his death as an act of atonement and may even have thought of Isaiah's suffering Servant—one who was punished by God for the sake of the Old Testament community of faith. In this matter it is crucial to note that the LXX version of Isa 53:12 is "He himself bore the sins of many and was handed over for the sake of their sins"[222] while the Hebrew text reads: "He bore the sins of many, and made intercessions for the transgressors."

As indicated above, the creedal formula "Jesus died for us" (5:10) belongs to pre-Pauline Greek Christianity. In the preceding section 4:13–17, it may have helped Paul to express the means of uniting the Christians with Jesus at his second coming (through Jesus—because of Jesus' death for the Christians). In the present section Paul uses it to explain how it is that Christians whether dead or alive will once again be united with Jesus. As one can see, Christianity at that time was still "inchoate and various."[223]

5:10 "Together with" recalls the end of 4:17 and, as it does there, designates the heavenly fellowship of both the survivors and those raised at the time of

Christ's return. "To be awake" and "to sleep" are not to be taken as in vv. 6–7, where they designate morality. Here, referring back to 4:13–18, they relate to Christians who are still alive and those who have died, and once again attest that both groups will be saved at the imminent second coming.

5:11 The similar content of this and 4:18 makes it clear that v. 11 points back to 4:13–18. And since Paul thus emphasizes the close relationship between 4:13–18 and 5:1–11, v. 11 can be seen as a transition to the next section.

I THESSALONIANS 5:12–22
Exhortations of the Community

[12]But we ask you, brothers, to respect those

> who labor among you
> and govern you in the Lord
> and admonish you,

and to esteem them very highly in love because of their work.

> [13]Be at peace among yourselves.

[14a]And we exhort you, brothers,

> [14b]admonish the disorderly,
> [14c]encourage the despondent,
> [14d]help the weak,
> [14e]be patient with them all.

> [15]See that none of you repays evil (*kakon*) for evil (*kakon*),
> but always seek to do good (*agathon*) to one another and to all.

> [16]Rejoice always,
> [17]pray constantly,
> [18a]give thanks in all circumstances.

[18b]For this is the will of God in Christ Jesus for you.

> [19]Do not extinguish the Spirit,
> [20]do not spurn prophesying,
> [21]but examine everything;
> hold fast what is good,
> [22]abstain from all forms of evil (*ponêron*).

5:12 The triad of activities "to labor," "to govern," and "to admonish" does not characterize three groups of persons, but designates "the same human beings along with three aspects of their work."[224] It is too early in the community tradition for individuals to have been assigned special offices or functions, but this will change later on.[225]

5:13 "Love" echoes the same noun in v. 8. Paul affirms the demand, which in v. 12 he had expressed by the verb "to respect." The exhortation that the Thessalonians be at peace among themselves belongs to the stream of Jewish admonitions of which Christian ethics is one part:

> Live at peace with all human beings! (Rom 12:18b)
> Live in peace! (2 Cor 13:11)
> Be at peace with one another! (Mark 9:50)

With the call to peace, Mark seems to hark back to the starting point of the dispute between the disciples in vv. 33–34, but draws the moral from an element of tradition that was inserted.[226] Thus the peace saying in Mark 9:50 derives from Mark and not from the historical Jesus. See further Sir 6:6; Matt 5:9; 1 Pet 3:10–11 (= Ps 34:15); Jas 3:18.

5:14 The last of these four imperatives sums up the first three. The pronoun "all" at v. 14e includes non-Christians, for in v. 15a it is used in this sense. Only here (v. 14e) in the New Testament is the word "despondent"[227] employed. "Weak" (v. 14d) refers to sickness of either the body or the soul. The style is liturgical. Confer the following prayer from Rome as a parallel:

> We ask you, O Master,
> to be our helper and defender.
>
> Save those of us who are in affliction,
> show mercy to those who are humble,
> raise those who have fallen,
> show yourself to those who are in need,
> heal those who are sick.
> set straight those among your people who are going astray.
>
> Feed the hungry,
> ransom out prisoners,
> raise up the weak,
> encourage the despondent (*oligopsychountas*).
>
> Let all the nations know you,
> That you alone are God,
> That Jesus Christ is your child,
> And that we are your people
> And the sheep of your pasture. (1 Clem 59:4[228])

5:15a The command not to repay evil for evil is found verbatim in Rom 12:17a and 1 Pet 3:9a. The saying does not derive from the historical Jesus.

See further Matt 5:39a: "But I say to you, Do not resist evil!" Yet Matthew has invented this logion of Jesus along with Matt 5:38: "You have heard that it was said, An eye for an eye, a tooth for a tooth." Thus vv. 38–39a are a construction of Matthew analogous to the antitheses that precede it.[229] Matthew has created them, like the third (and the sixth) for the purpose of instruction.

Note that these sayings from Paul's letters and from the gospel of Matthew reject the *ius talionis*[230] that had already been repudiated by Jewish teachers:

> Do not say, I will repay evil; wait for the Lord, and he will help you. (Prov 20:22)

> Do not say, I will do to him as he has done to me; I will pay back the person for what he has done. (Prov 24:29)

> [1]The vengeful person will face the vengeance of the Lord, who keeps strict account of his sins. [2]Forgive your neighbor his wrongdoing; then, when you pray, your sins will be forgiven. . . . [7]Think of the commandments and do not be enraged at your neighbor; think of the covenant of the Most High, and overlook faults. (Sir 28:1–2, 7)

5:15b The saying, "Always seek to do good," has two parallels in Paul's letters: Rom 2:10 and Gal 6:10. Note that Paul does not attribute it to Jesus.

5:16–18 The section contains three admonitions: a) to rejoice always; b) to pray constantly; c) to give thanks in all circumstances.

5:16 The adverb "always" picks up the same word from v. 15. On the imperative to rejoice cf. 1 Thess 1:6; 2:19, 20; 3:9; see further Phil 2:17b.

5:17 On the charge to pray constantly cf. Rom 1:9–10; 12:12. This corresponds to Paul's statement that he always remembers the community in his prayers.

5:18 Prayer and thanksgiving are connected in Paul's thought; cf. 2 Cor 1:11; Phil 4:6. "For this is the will of God," repeats 1 Thess 4:3 verbatim, but here it is supplemented by "in Christ Jesus" to indicate both the context and the validity of the three admonitions.

5:19–20 Paul here deals with the spiritual phenomena of speaking in tongues and prophecy. 1 Corinthians 12–14 shows what the apostle means. He encourages his readers not to curtail tongues and prophecy but rather to practice both as long as they give evidence of their authenticity. That one must not quench the Spirit (v. 19) means that enthusiasm should be given all due freedom of expression.[231]

5:21 In the context of the letter the apostle is calling for an examination[232] of spiritual practices, but at the same time he seems to be presenting a philosophical motto. Note the parallel at Rom 12:2b in which Paul speaks about "the renewal of your mind, that you may examine (*dokimazō*) what is the will of God, what is good and acceptable and perfect."

5:22 By cleverly linking the negative imperative "abstain from" (*apechesthai*) to the affirmative imperative "hold fast" (*katechein*) in v. 21b by means of lexical contrast and aural similarity, Paul emphasizes the content of both of these closing adjurations.

I THESSALONIANS 5:23–28

Final Wishes and Greetings

[23]May the God of peace himself sanctify you wholly,
may your spirit
and soul
and body be preserved whole,
blameless at the coming of our Lord Jesus Christ.

[24]He who calls you is faithful,
and he will also do [this].

[25]Brothers, pray for us.
[26]Greet all the brothers with a sacred kiss.
[27]I adjure you by the Lord that this letter be read to all the
brothers.

[28]The grace of our Lord Jesus Christ be with you.

5:23 In his extant authentic letters Paul employs the phrase "God of peace" five times.[233] In v. 23a he echoes 5:13, where he admonishes the community to have peace among themselves, and 5:3, where he utilizes the slogan "peace and security" to describe the political propaganda of the Roman Empire and predicts its destruction in the near future. It may be that the phrase "God of peace" in this verse has a political undertone, and that characteristic is likely true for the use of "God of peace" in Rom 16:20,[234] where Paul predicts that the God of peace will soon crush Satan under the feet of the Roman Christians.[235]

The division of the human being into spirit, soul and body is in tension with Paul's usual division of human life into flesh and spirit.[236] But the present triad occurs in the context of a traditional prayer, and Paul uses it to express his hope that the community will do well until Jesus' second coming.[237] Further, Paul's use of the words "wholly"[238] and "whole"[239] indicate that his wording is dependent on a liturgical piece.

5:24 The sentence is a liturgical assurance of God's trustworthiness,[240] and its placement at the end of the letter is deliberate.

The three final verses contain three commands and a closing benediction of grace.

5:25 On Paul's wish that the Thessalonians pray for him, cf. v. 17 and Rom 15:30. See further the earlier reassurance (1:2) that Paul prays for the

Thessalonians. Once again as often before, we find the theme of reciprocity between apostle and community, this time in the context of prayer.

5:26 The injunction to greet one another with a "sacred kiss" appears four times in Paul's authentic letters[241] and once using the phrase "kiss of love" in the pseudepigraphical 1 Peter (5:14a). It may be a step too far to distinguish between "all the brothers"[242] found in 1 Thessalonians and "one another"[243] used in the other four cases, but it could be that the latter usage became a standard variation of the phrase Paul used in his first letter. In short, one is permitted to wonder whether the kiss of peace first enjoined in 1 Thessalonians evolved into an accepted symbol of Christian communal life.[244] Indeed, Paul himself may have introduced a sacred kiss "as the mode of greeting among believers."[245]

5:27 The peremptory tone of Paul's demand that the letter be read to everyone is surprising. Ferdinand Christian Baur concluded from this the non-authenticity of the letter.[246] A better explanation for this phenomenon is that Paul establishes a precedent, and his strict order to read the letter to the entire community—likely during a gathering for worship—is "related to the peculiar character of 1 Thessalonians, [which] is the first letter to a newly founded community without much tradition."[247] Besides, Paul's adjuration "is an implicit assertion of his authority over the congregation."[248]

5:28 In his closing, Paul echoes the introductory invocation found in 1:1c–d (though here he omits mention of God the Father), and thus symbolically frames his oldest extant letter with the promise of divine grace.

Notes

1. Boyarin, *A Radical Jew*, claims that "Paul's letters are addressed to us—to me as a (post)modern Jew" (228). But of course are they not addressed to us. My impression is that what Boyarin ultimately does amounts to about the same as what I do in the present book when I "evaluate" what Paul has done. See "Understanding Paul" (Chapter 1).

2. Cf. Marxsen, *Der erste Brief*, 9.

3. Silvanus (in Acts always "Silas") was a companion of Paul during his missionary activities in Europe and a co-founder of the congregations of Thessalonica and of Corinth (2 Cor 1:19). He may have been at home in Jerusalem (Acts 15:22, 27, 32) or in Antioch (Acts 15:40). Note Silvanus' appearance in 1 Pet 5:12 ("faithful brother").

4. Timothy of Derbe (Acts 16:1) was one of Paul's most important co-workers, and also served as his envoy (1 Cor 4:13). He was active in Philippi, Thessalonica, and Corinth. In addition to multiple references in 1 Thessalonians, he is listed as the co-sender of three Pauline letters: 2 Corinthians, Philippians and Philemon. He is also named as co-sender of the inauthentic letters 2 Thessalonians and Colossians, and is, of course, the addressee of the forged epistles 1 and 2 Timothy.

5. See the more detailed discussion under "Authenticity" (Chapter 2).

6. Rom 1:7; 1 Cor 1:2; 2 Cor 1:1; Gal 1:2; Phil 1:1.

7. See Col 4:16; 2 Thess 1:1.

8. Acts 19:32, 39–40.

9. Cf. Crüsemann, *Die pseudepigraphen Briefe*, 236.

10. 1 Thess 2:14; 1 Cor 1:2; 11:22; 15:9; 2 Cor 1:1. Cf. Phil 3:6 where *ekklēsia* has no specific addition.

11. Rom 16:16 ("all the communities of Christ").

12. Deut 23:2–3: [2]No bastard shall be admitted to the congregation (*ekklēsia*) of the Lord. Even to the tenth generation, none of their descendants shall be admitted to the congregation (*ekklēsia*) of the Lord. [3]No Ammonite or Moabite shall be admitted to the congregation (*ekklēsia*) of the Lord. Even to the tenth generation, none of their descendants shall be admitted to the congregation (*ekklēsia*) of the Lord.

13. Conzelmann, *An Outline*, 35.

14. But cf. 1 Thess 2:2; Rom 5:17; 5:11.

15. Dibelius, *An die Thessalonicher*, 2; Strecker, *Theology of the New Testament*, 117–23 ("The Formula 'In Christ'").

16. Dibelius, *An die Thessalonicher*, 2.

17. *agapētoi theou* (Rom 1:7). See 1 Thess 1:4: "brothers beloved by God."

18. 1 Cor 1:2; 2 Cor 2:1.

19. Rom 1:5; 5:2, 15, 17, 20–21; 2 Cor 6:1; Gal 5:4. Cf. Bultmann, *Theology of the New Testament*, vol. 1: 288–92 ("§32. Grace as event").

20. Rom 6:17; 7:25; 1 Cor 15:57; 2 Cor 8:16; 9:15.

21. 2 Cor 8:1, 4, 6–7, 9, 19. In 1 Cor 16:1 the collection is called *logeia*, in Rom 15:26 *koinōnia*. For other designations of the collection such as *logeia*, *koinōnia*, and *diakonia* see the survey in Georgi, *Remembering the Poor*, 196–97.

22. Cf. Acts 15:23; 23:26; Jas 1:1.

23. 1 Thess 5:28.

24. 2 Baruch stems from the early second century ce but its traditions, such as the letter of "Baruch" (see above), are older. Translation following Charlesworth, *The Old Testament Pseudepigrapha*, 648 (A. F. J. Klijn).

25. But see Col 1:2b: "Grace to you and peace from God, our Father."

26. On 1 Thess 1:2–3:10 as *one* long thanksgiving see the discussion under "Authenticity" (Chapter 2).

27. Rom 5:1–5; 1 Cor 13:13; 1 Thess 5:8; cf. Col 1:4–5. See further Lüdemann, *Paul: The Founder of Christianity*, 104–7.

28. Cf. Laub, *1. und 2. Thessalonicherbrief*, 16.

29. 1 Thess 2:1, 9, 14, 17; 3:7, 10, 13; 4:1, 10; 5:1, 4, 12, 14, 25. Cf. 5:26, 27.

30. See already "Unique Features" (Chapter 2).

31. Cf. Deut 7:6: "The Lord your God has chosen you to be a people for his own possession, out of all peoples that are on the face of this earth."

32. Sanders, *Paul and Palestinian Judaism*, 87.

33. Apart from the present passage, "election" occurs in the Pauline letters in Rom 9:11; 11:5, 7; 11:28. The adjective "elected" appears only in Rom 8:33; 16:13; cf. Col 3:12. The verb "to elect" is used in 1 Cor 1:27–28; cf. Eph 1:4.

34. Furnish, *1 Thessalonians*, 43.

35. Cf. 1 Thess 2:12; 4:7; 5:24.

36. Cf. Ps 144:13a (LXX): "The Lord is faithful in all his words and holy in all his deeds." See further Deut 7:9: "The Lord your God is God, the faithful God."

37. On God's faithfulness see 1 Thess 5:24.

38. Marxsen, *Der erste Brief*, 37.

39. *mimêtai*.

40. *typos*.

41. *symmimêtai mou ginesthe*.

42. *echete typon hêmas*.

43. 1 Thess 1:6; 2:14; 1 Cor 4:16; 11:1; Phil 3:17.

44. Cf. Betz, *Nachfolge*, 84–101.

45. Cf. Matt 16:24–28.

46. Cf. 1 Thess 4:3–8; 5:13–18; Rom 12:8–10.

47. Cf. Ehrman, *New Testament*, 42–45.

48. Cf. Betz, *Nachfolge*, 173.

49. Sanders, *Paul and Palestinian Judaism*, 87.

50. Cf. 1 Thess 3:4: "When we were with you, we told you beforehand that we were to suffer affliction; and as you know, it has come to pass." On this, see the interpretive note on 3:4 below.

51. Cf. Matt 24:9a: "Then they will deliver you up to affliction, and put you to death."

52. Cf. Mark 13:14: "But when you see 'the abomination of desolation' [Dan 12:1; 11:31] standing where it should not—let the reader note—then those in Judea should flee to the mountains."

53. Cf. Dan 12:1: "At that time Michael, the great prince, the protector of your people, shall arise. There shall be a time of anguish, such as has never occurred since nations first came into existence. But at that time your people shall be delivered, everyone who is found written in the book." (NRSV)

54. Cf. Volz, *Die Eschatologie*, 147–63 (§31: "The Final Evil Time").

55. *eishodos* (1:9/2:1).

56. In Gal 1:13–14, 23 Paul similarly quotes traditions about himself. The Galatians to whom the letter is addressed and the Christians persecuted by Paul had heard and transmitted these traditions.

57. V. 9: to turn to (*epistrephô*); true (*alêthinos*); to serve God (*douleuô theô*); v. 10: to wait for (*anamenô*); from the dead (*ek nekrôn*); wrath to come (*orgê hê erchomenê*).

58. Mark 1:4. This piece of information comes from tradition and is historical. Cf. Lüdemann, *Jesus after 2000 Years*, 7–8.

59. The concern that his work may have been in vain Paul repeats in 1 Thess 3:5 and in other letters (Gal 2:5; Phil 2:16) reiterates. This motive echoes Isa 49:4; 65:23.

60. *oidate*.

61. Cf. 1 Thess 1:5.

62. Cf. 1 Thess 2:2, 5, 11.

63. Acts 16:20b–21: "These men disturb our city; they are Jews and advocate customs that are not lawful for us as Romans to adopt or to observe."

64. Translation following Malherbe, *The Letters to the Thessalonians*, 3.

65. Phil 1:30.

66. Cf. Lüdemann, *Opposition to Paul*, 64–111.

67. Luke 10:7. The parallel in Matthew's gospel varies just a little: "The laborer is wealthy of his *food*."

68. For more detailed discussion, see Lüdemann, *Opposition to Paul*, 65–72.

69. Dibelius, *An die Thessalonicher*, 7–11. I use "popular philosopher" as an umbrella term for teachers in the first two centuries ce like Musonius Rufus, Epictetus, Dio Chrysostomos, and those first-century ce Cynics who were preoccupied with ethical matters.

70. Malherbe, *The Letters to the Thessalonians*, 133–66. This commentary builds on various smaller books by Malherbe listed in the bibliography.

71. The text is also printed in Malherbe, *Paul and the Thessalonians*, 3–4.

72. Adapted from Malherbe, *Paul and the Thessalonians*, 4.

73. *parrhēziazesthai*. On the noun *parrhēsia* ("free expression"), cf. 2 Cor 7:4; Phlm 8; 2 Cor 3:12; Phil 1:20.

74. *planē, akatharsia, dolos.*

75. Malherbe, *Paul and the Popular Philosophers*, 47.

76. Malherbe, *Paul and the Popular Philosophers*, 46–47.

77. Malherbe, *Paul and the Popular Philosophers*, 46–47.

78. Cf. Lüdemann, *Paul—Apostle to the Gentiles*, 51–52.

79. 1 Cor 10:33; Rom 15:2.

80. 1 Cor 7:33–34; Gal 1:10.

81. *kolakeia.*

82. Cf. Malherbe, *The Letters to the Thessalonians*, 159.

83. Cf. Dio Chrysostomos, *Discourses* 32.10–11.

84. *ēpios.* The ancient manuscripts vary between *ēpios* (gentle) and *nēpios* (childlike). Because of the context, the reading can only be *ēpios.*

85. Malherbe, *Moral Exhortation*, 152 (fragment of Musonius Rufus, the teacher of Dio Chrysostomos).

86. The translation mostly follows Koester, *History, Culture and Religion*, 344.

87. Koester, *History, Culture and Religion*, 344.

88. Cf. Malherbe, *Paul and the Popular Philosophers*, 53.

89. Malherbe, *Paul and the Popular Philosophers*, 58.

90. Malherbe, *Paul and the Popular Philosophers*, 59.

91. Malherbe, *Paul and the Popular Philosophers*, 66.

92. Gal 2:20.

93. 2 Cor 5:17. See further Deissmann, *Paul*, 140.

94. Cf. Gal 3:26–28.

95. Cf. Rom 6:4; see further Col 2:12.

96. Cf. 1 Thess 4:13–17 and the accompanying interpretive notes below.

97. 1 Thess 4:17; 5:10.

98. 1 Cor 9:22. See Chadwick, "'All Things to All Men'"; Rudolph, *A Jew to Jews*, 1–19.

99. *logos akoēs par' hēmōn tou theou.*

100. *logos tou theou.*

101. *logos akoēs.*

102. Cf. Holtz, *Der erste Brief*, 98.

103. Cf. in Rom 15:31 "the unbelievers in Judea" (*hoi apeithountes en Ioudaia*) as a reference to non-believing Jews who may attack Paul on his way to Jerusalem to deliver the collection.

104. Mark 14–15; Matthew 26–27; Luke 22–23; John 18–19.

105. Mark 14:53–65; 15:1; Matt 26:57–68; 27:1–2; Luke 22:66–71; 23:1; John 18:12–13, 24, 28.

106. Acts 3:15; 4:10; 7:52.

107. Cf. Jer 26:20–23. See further Jer 20:1–2 (Jeremiah was almost killed).

108. For further details see Scott, "Paul's Use of Deuteronomic Tradition," 647–50. The basic book on the subject is Steck, *Israel*.

109. The process of assigning words to Jesus can be observed in the letters to the seven churches in Revelation 2–3 which "Jesus" dictated to John. On this see Lüdemann, *What Jesus Didn't Say*, 120–29; Boring, *The Continuing Voice of Jesus*, passim.

110. Lüdemann, *Jesus after 2000 Years*, 81–82.

111. Davies, *Jewish and Pauline Studies*, 126: "A comparison of Mark 12:1b–5, 7, 8, 9 with 1 Thess 2:15, 16 reveals a common sequence of thought."

112. Cf. Mark 11:27; 12:1. Mark 12:1b–9 contains no prediction of the annihilation of all non-believing Jews.

113. Cf. the reference to the charge of "pleasing" people in 1 Thess 2:4.

114. Conzelmann, *Gentiles—Jews—Christians*, 118–19. Note that although Tacitus' work postdates 1 Thessalonians, the polemic described by him is older than that in Paul's letter.

115. The accusation of *misanthrôpia* was later used against the Christians in connection with the burning of half of Rome in 64 ce. See Tacitus, *Annals* 15.44.4 with the comments of Schäfer, *Judeophobia*, 190–91.

116. Conzelmann, *Gentiles—Jews—Christians*; Schäfer, *Judeophobia*.

117. On Apollonius Molon cf. Conzelmann, *Gentiles—Jews—Christians*, 77–79.

118. On Hecataeus of Abdera cf. Conzelmann, *Gentiles—Jews—Christians*, 60–62; Schäfer, *Judeophobia*, 15–17.

119. Cf. Conzelmann, *Gentiles—Jews—Christians*, 151–52.

120. 1 Cor 15:9; Gal 1:13, 23; Phil 3:6.

121. Donfried, *Paul, Thessalonica, and Early Christianity*, 202–3.

122. Gal 5:11.

123. Cf. Deut 25:3.

124. Ps 11:6; Ps 23:5.

125. Furnish, *1 Thessalonians*, 71.

126. Dibelius, *An die Thessalonicher*, 12, referring to Matt 12:28: "But if I cast out demons by the spirit of God, the kingdom of God has come (*ephthasen*) upon you." Schlueter, *Filling up the Measure*, 56, disagrees: "The use of *ephthasen* in 1 Thess. 2:16c is not a sentence with a conditional clause [as in Matt 12:28]; rather it stands on its own, and to translate it as a proleptic would be an anomaly in the New Testament."

127. In Greek, *ephthasen de autous hê orgê tou theou eis telos*.

128. Schlueter, *Filling up the Measure*, 22. See further Frame, *A Critical and Exegetical Commentary*, 115–16. An English translation of the Testament of Levi can be found in Charlesworth, *The Old Testament Pseudepigrapha*, 788–95 (Howard Kee).

129. The participial construction cannot be reproduced in the translation.

130. The verb "to hinder" is also found in Rom 1:13; 1 Cor 14:39, the verb "to

speak" is found 52 times in Paul (cf. especially 1 Thess 2:2, 4). "Gentiles" is used by Paul 45 times and "to save" 19 times.

131. Phil 2:6–11, expanded in v. 8b by "to death on the cross"; Rom 3:25–26, expanded in v. 25 "through faith"; Gal 3:26–28, expanded in v. 26 by "through faith." For further details, see Strecker, *Theology of the New Testament*, 64–78.

132. Broer, "Antijudaismus," 330.

133. Cf. Crüsemann, *Die pseudepigraphen Briefe*, 49–56 ("Elements of Ancient pagan anti-Semitism").

134. Thus Schlueter, *Filling up the Measure*, 187: "(T)he hostile statements . . . indicate an ongoing relationship—in this case a conflict—between Jews." Similarly Kampling. "Skizze," 185–86 following Schreckenberg, *Texte*, 133.

135. Schlueter, *Filling up the Measure*, 186.

136. *Pace* Furnish, *1 Thessalonians*, 73, where the inclusion of Gentile anti-Judaism in Paul's polemic is overlooked. With respect to assessing Paul's polemic, Furnish overall follows Schlueter, *Filling up the Measure*.

137. See the interpretive note on 1 Thess 5:9–10.

138. Schlueter, *Filling up the Measure*, 197.

139. Cf. 2 Cor 10:1; Phlm 9.

140. *pros kairon hōras* means "at the time in question" and not "for a short period of time." See Hurd, *The Earlier Letters*, 107.

141. Cf. Schlier, *Der Apostel und seine Gemeinde*, 46.

142. Donfried, *Paul, Thessalonica, and Early Christianity*, xxxvi, denies that Timothy and Silas were ever with Paul in Athens. This serves to harmonize Acts (17:14–15) with Paul and seems not to be the most plausible meaning of 3:2. Cf. Holtz, *Der erste Brief*, 124.

143. Schade, *Apokalyptische Christologie*, 127.

144. Holtz, *Der erste Brief*, 136.

145. Cf. Konradt, *Gericht und Gemeinde*, 93 n. 413.

146. Thus Rigaux, *Saint Paul: Les Epîtres aux Thessaloniciens*, 491–92.

147. Cf. Zech 14:5 (LXX); Job 1:5; 15:15; Ps 88 (89):6; Tob 11:14; 12:5; 1 Hen 1:9 (quoted in Jude 14).

148. Cf. Dobschütz, *Die Thessalonicher-Briefe*, 155.

149. Cf. Sanders, *Paul*, 113.

150. Best, *A Commentary*, 162–63.

151. Cf. Bauer, *A Greek-English Lexicon*, 761 b.2.

152. Furnish, *1 Thessalonians*, 89–90.

153. 1 Cor 5:10; 6:9–10; Gal 5:19–21. Cf. Mark 7:21; 1 Pet 4:3.

154. *hyperbainō*. The verb occurs only here in the New Testament.

155. *pleonekteō*. Cf. 1 Thess 2:5.

156. Cf. Lünemann, *Kritisch exegetisches Handbuch*, 108.

157. *pleonexia*. Cf. 1 Thess 2:5.

158. Cf. 1 Cor 5:10–11; 6:9–10.

159. Cf. Holtz, *Der erste Brief*, 168.

160. Ps 93:1 (LXX): "The God of vengeance is Lord. The God of vengeance has openly expressed himself."

161. Konradt, *Gericht und Gemeinde*, 97.

162. *akatharsia.*

163. The same antithesis can be found Rom 6:19: "For just as you once yielded your members to *uncleanness* and to greater and greater iniquity, so now yield your members to righteousness for *sanctification.*"

164. Verse 8 may be called a "sentence of holy law" and should be added to the list in Käsemann, *New Testament Questions*, 66–81 ("Sentences of Holy Law in the New Testament"). Käsemann deals there with 1 Cor 3:17; 5:3–5; 14:37–38; 16:22; Gal 1:9.

165. Laub, *Eschatologische Verkündigung*, 61 n. 56.

166. See Isa 54:13a: "All your children shall be taught by the Lord." Cf. John 6:45.

167. Cf. Malherbe, *The Letters to the Thessalonians*, 248–49.

168. Cf. Laub, *Eschatologische Verkündigung*, 175.

169. *euschêmonôs*

170. Cf. Söding, *Die Trias Glaube*, 91.

171. Cf. 1 Cor 5:1–5.

172. Cf. 1 Cor 3:16; 6:19.

173. Cf. Lev 19:2.

174. Nock, *St. Paul*, 235. See further Dewey et al., *The Authentic Letters*, 7, 159–62 ("Paul and Rhetoric"), 257–59 ("Paul and Diatribe").

175. Nock, *St. Paul*, 234–35.

176. Nock, *St. Paul*, 236.

177. In the following exegesis I have used material from Lüdemann, *Paul—Apostle to the Gentiles*, 213–37.

178. Cf. Rom 1:13; 11:25; 1 Cor 10:1; 12:1; 2 Cor 1:8. Cf. 1 Cor 11:3; Phil 1:12.

179. Cf. 1 Thess 1:10b; 1 Cor 15:3–5; Rom 4:24–25; 6:4, 9; 10:9; Luke 23:34.

180. Cf. further Rom 14:9 with explanations in Lüdemann, *Paul—Apostle to the Gentiles*, 215. However, Donfried, *Paul, Thessalonica, and Early Christianity*, 82, thinks that the phrase "Jesus dies and rose" undoubtedly is a pre-Pauline formula since Paul consistently uses the verb *egeirô* instead of *anistêmi.*"

181. Donfried, *Paul, Thessalonica, and Early Christianity*, 82.

182. Marxsen, "Auslegung," 29.

183. *en logô kyriou.*

184. Luz, *Das Geschichtsverständnis*, 327, lists the following passages from the New Testament that have been cited as parallels up to now: Matt 10:39; 16:25, 28; 24:31, 34; 25:6; 26:64; Luke 13:30; John 5:25; 6:39–40.

185. Against Jeremias, *Unknown Sayings*, 82.

186. Cf. Boring, *The Continuing Voice of Jesus*, 61–64.

187. *logos kyriou* does not necessarily designate a single saying. See Bauer, *A Greek-English Lexicon*, 478–80.

188. Bultmann, *The History of the Synoptic Tradition*, 122.

189. For further details see Lüdemann, *Paul—Apostle to the Gentiles*, 222.

190. On the theological concept of the "remnant" cf. Isa 10:22; Hos 2:11; Rom 9:27; 11:5. See further Munck, *Christ and Israel*, 111–16.

191. Paul does not say anything about the state of the dead. Although it would have been appropriate at this point to say something about their present fellowship with Christ, Paul had not yet arrived at this form of hope at the time of 1 Thessalonians. The reason for it seemed to be that survival was the rule and that his hope was still exclusively focused on the notion of the *parousia.* Phil 1:23 differs here.

192. But see the creed in 1 Thess 5:10 for the theological concept that the death of Christ "for us" ensures the future union of the believers with Christ. See the interpretive note on 1 Thess 5:9–10 below.

193. Schlueter, *Filling up the Measure*, 106.

194. Cf. Marxsen, "Auslegung," 31.

195. See Enoch (Gen 5:24); Elijah (1 Kgs 2:11).

196. In this section I have used material from Lüdemann, *Paul—Apostle to the Gentiles*, 227–30.

197. Translation following Charlesworth, *The Old Testament Pseudepigrapha*, 551–53 (Bruce M. Metzger).

198. Translation following Charlesworth, *The Old Testament Pseudepigrapha*, 538 (Bruce M. Metzger).

199. Dibelius, *An die Thessalonicher*, 27.

200. Volz, *Die Eschatologie*, 136.

201. Translation following Charlesworth, *The Old Testament Pseudepigrapha*, 631 (A. F. J. Klijn).

202. Translation following Charlesworth, *The Old Testament Pseudepigrapha*, 638–39 (A. F. J. Klijn).

203. Translation following Charlesworth, *The Old Testament Pseudepigrapha*, 533 (Bruce M. Metzger).

204. Translation following Charlesworth, *The Old Testament Pseudepigrapha*, 552 (Bruce M. Metzger).

205. *peri.*

206. Cf. its earlier use in 4:9 and 4:13.

207. Cf. Matt 24:36; Mark 13:32; Acts 1:7.

208. Cf. 1 Thess 4:9.

209. Cf. Harnisch, *Eschatologische Existenz*, 84–116 ("The Use of the Image of the 'Thief' in Early Christian Literature").

210. Cf. Laub, *Eschatologische Verkündigung*, 158.

211. On the image of a pregnant woman cf. Isa 26:17 (negative); Isa 66:7–9 (positive).

212. Konradt, *Gericht und Gemeinde*, 71.

213. Lindemann, "Christliche Gemeinden und das Römische Reich," 116; cf. Ehrhardt, *Politische Metaphysik*, 20–21; Crossan and Reed, *In Search of Paul*; Harrison, *Paul and the Imperial Authorities*.

214. Cf. Rom 13:1–7. See further Lohse, *Paulus*, 237, who rightly emphasizes that Rom 13:1–7 does not contain a single word to be called specifically Christian. It reflects the teachings of Hellenistic Judaism.

215. Cf. Gal 3:26–28.

216. Cf. 1 Pet 5:8: "Be sober, be watchful."

217. Konradt, *Gericht und Gemeinde*, 173.

218. Cf. Rom 4:25; 8:32; 1 Cor 11:24; 15:3; Gal 1:4, etc.

219. Cf. Lüdemann, "The First Three Years of Christianity," 37–38; Lüdemann, *Die ersten drei Jahre Christentum*, 101–2.

220. Versnel, "Making Sense of Jesus' Death," 234–39.

221. See 2 Macc 7:32–33, 37–38; 4 Macc 6:27–29.

222. Cf. Rom 4:25: "He was put to death for the sake of our trespasses."

223. Riddle, *Paul—Man of Conflict*, 23–24.

224. Dobschütz, *Die Thessalonicher-Briefe*, 215.

225. Cf. 1 Tim 5:17: "Let the Elders who rule well be considered worthy of double honor, especially those who labor in preaching and teaching."

226. Vv. 44 and 46 do not belong to the original text of the Gospel of Mark.

227. *oligopsychos.*

228. Translation following Ehrman, *Apostolic Fathers I*, 143.

229. The six antitheses (Matt 5:21–48) are of varying length, and address traditional and "new" views on killing, adultery, divorce, swearing, non-violence and love of enemy.

230. Cf. Exod 21:23–24; Lev 24:19–20; Deut 19:21.

231. Cf. Marxsen, *Der erste Brief*, 72.

232. The verb is *dokimazô.*

233. Rom 15:33; 16:20; 2 Cor 13:11; Phil 3:9.

234. Cf. Lohse, *Der Brief an die Römer*, 414.

235. Cf. Rev 20:1–10. On Satan as a designation of Rome cf. Revelation 13; 17.

236. Cf. "flesh and spirit" in 1 Cor 2:14–15; 15:44, 46.

237. Cf. 1 Thess 3:13; 4:13–18.

238. *holoteleis.*

239. *holoklêron.*

240. Cf. Deut 7:9; Psalms of Solomon 14:1; 1 Cor 10:13; 2 Cor 1:18.

241. Rom 16:16; 1 Cor 16:20; 2 Cor 13:12; 1 Thess 5:23.

242. *adelphous panta*s.

243. *allêlous.*

244. Judaism does not know the rite of the holy kiss (cf. Feldmeier, *The First Letter of Peter*, 256); see further Klassen, "The Sacred Kiss;" Ebel, *Die Attraktivität*, 212–13 n. 188.

245. Furnish, *1 Thessalonians*, 125.

246. Baur, *Paulus*, vol. 2, 106–7.

247. Holtz, *Der erste Brief*, 273.

248. Furnish, *1 Thessalonians*, 126.

Appendix 1

A Pauline Chronology[1]

Explanatory Note

I have several times dealt with the chronology of Paul[2] in an attempt to familiarize readers with the American scholar John Knox, whose studies in this field during the 1930s[3] not only constitute a solid body of historical work, but even more important, offer a new understanding of Early Christianity and of Paul's role in its development. Few exegetical publications merit the applause that those of John Knox richly deserve. He rigorously followed the sound and widely accepted rule that it is Paul's own letters that must guide any attempt to understand his thought and reconstruct his chronology. One of the more significant results of his analyses was to date Paul's earliest extant letter, 1 Thessalonians, about ten years earlier than the commonly assumed date.

A significant minority of American exegetes continues to follow Knox's chronology, while in Germany its acceptance seems to have decreased.[4]

Yet more strange is that many American scholars who are familiar with Knox's chronology seem to think it not worthy of mention. In most cases the reader learns that 1 Thessalonians is "usually" dated around 50 CE, while neither the name nor the argument of the scholar who placed it a decade earlier is given.[5]

Because of this unsatisfactory situation I have once again undertaken the task of making the case for Knox' chronology, for it presents the clearest and cleanest way to make sense of the available sources and has been too easily dismissed by those led astray by the canonical weight of Acts. I can only hope that my American colleagues will come to recognize that Knox' work on Paul's chronology was a major twentieth-century breakthrough, and that even F. C. Baur's highly regarded studies on the historical Paul and Acts failed to produce the long overdue revolution in Pauline chronology. Indeed, Baur did not try to establish a chronology, perhaps because he regarded 1 Thessalonians and Philippians as inauthentic and thus lacked a satisfactory array of sources to support such a construct. It was not until Knox made his detailed analysis of the relationship between Paul's letters and Acts that he was able to date 1 Thessalonians within the first decade of the Christian movement and thus provide the basis for the exegeses in this book.

Let me hasten to add that my work on Pauline chronology aims at more than determining the various dates pertaining to Paul's life and writings, for I shall attempt both to arrange his activities in their proper sequence and to explain why events occurred as they did.

THE OLD CHRONOLOGY AND ITS PROBLEMS

The conventional view of Paul's life is the result of attempts to conflate statements in Acts with information contained in the letters. A general agreement of scholars has long held that these two sources may be harmonized by proceeding from the sole absolute datum found in the reference to the governor Gallio in Acts 18:12.[6] Gallio, the half-brother of the philosopher Seneca, held office in 51–52 CE.

Further corroboration is claimed on the basis of Acts 18:2, which reports that Priscilla and Aquila had recently arrived in Corinth from Rome after the expulsion of the Jews—an event dated to 49 CE on the basis of a fifth-century Christian source.

Since these two dates confirm one another, and especially as Acts 18:11 narrates that Paul stood trial before Gallio eighteen months after his arrival in Corinth, scholars have generally concluded that Luke's report of Paul's *first* Corinthian mission is historically accurate. *Thus Paul was supposedly in Corinth as a Christian preacher for the first time around 50 CE.* With the date of the mission on European soil relatively secure, other dates are reckoned backward and forward from this period.

PERIOD SUBSEQUENT TO THE FOUNDING OF
THE CORINTHIAN CONGREGATION

After dwelling in Corinth, Paul traveled to Ephesus, then on to Palestine, and afterwards back to Ephesus.[7] There and in Macedonia, where he had gone after the stay at Ephesus,[8] Paul wrote the Corinthian letters or parts of them, and later returned to Jerusalem in order to deliver a collection.[9] The intention to raise money for the Jerusalem church[10] had been one of the most significant results of the so-called "Jerusalem conference," an earlier meeting between the Jewish Christian community of Jerusalem and the Gentile Christian churches represented by Paul and Barnabas.

PERIOD PRIOR TO THE FOUNDING OF THE
CORINTHIAN CONGREGATION

Based on the agreement of 1 Thessalonians 2–3 with Acts 17, it appears that before Paul's stay in Corinth he had done missionary work in Philippi, Thessalonica, and Athens. Prior to this mission—thus the traditional view— Paul had traveled to the Jerusalem conference as a delegate of the Antioch congregation and junior partner of Barnabas.

One can date that conference to fifteen years after Paul's conversion on the basis of the number of years in Gal 1:18 ("after three years," meaning "two years") and 2:1 ("after fourteen years," meaning "thirteen years"). Confirmation of this has commonly been derived from the references in both Acts 15:36–39 and Gal 2:11–14 to the conflict between Paul and Barnabas. For the fourteen years prior to the Jerusalem conference, Paul is supposed to have worked in Syria and Cilicia as a missionary of the Antioch congregation,[11] and it was only subsequent to a clash in Antioch after the conference[12] that Paul initiated the independent mission that took him ultimately as far as Greece.

OBJECTIONS

If this old chronology were correct, then all of Paul's letters would have been composed within a period of about three to four years. A veteran missionary who had already been a Christian for about nineteen years would thus have written all his known letters when he was between 53 and 56 years old.[13] Further, most of Paul's life as a Christian would have been spent during fourteen "silent" years in Syria and Cilicia.[14]

Yet looking back on his missionary work, he writes:

> [19b]Beginning from Jerusalem all around as far as to Illyricum I have completed the gospel of Christ, [20]thus considering it an honor not to preach the gospel where Christ had already been named, lest I build on another person's foundation. (Rom 15:19b–20)

It would be hard to reconcile with Paul's consciousness of himself as *the* apostle to the Gentiles[15] the idea that he had begun the mission in Europe only toward the end of his life, and years after the conference. Indeed, Paul would hardly have stayed "so long in what was really only a small part of the Graeco-Roman world if he had believed that . . . God's final judging and saving act was waiting till he should make an initial proclamation of the gospel in every nation."[16]

Furthermore, Paul was not a delegate representing Antioch at the Jerusalem conference, nor was he a junior colleague of Barnabas.[17] In Gal 2:2 Paul says that he traveled to Jerusalem as the result of a revelation, and in that same verse stresses his intention to present to the Jerusalem "pillars" the gospel that *he* preaches among the Gentiles. In the following verse he notes that he had taken Titus along with him to Jerusalem, a term that reflects Titus' inferiority to Paul, since in 2:1 he says that he went together with Barnabas and took along Titus. Thus he indicates both his equality with Barnabas and the lesser standing of Titus, an uncircumcised Greek who is never mentioned in Acts. Paul seems clearly intent on impressing the Galatians with his importance and his ability to challenge and even face down the august leaders of the Jerusalem community.

Regarding the old chronology, 49 CE is an uncertain date for the expulsion of the Jews from Rome, because it derives from a fifth-century Christian
source (Orosius) and is in conflict with earlier pagan authorities: The combined witness of Suetonius (early second century) and Dio Cassius (late second century) points to 41 CE as the date of the expulsion.[18]

In addition, Luke's references to incidents in world history are often false.
A few examples should suffice:[19]

1. Luke 1:5; 2:1–2: Luke mistakenly dates the birth of Jesus during
   the reign of Herod the Great (37 BCE–4 BCE) and at the time of the
   "worldwide" census of Quirinius. However, (a) the census of Quirinius
   occurred a decade after Herod's death,[20] and (b) Luke has a mistaken
   notion of the census, for it was limited to Judea and Syria.[21]

2. Luke 3:2 and Acts 4:6 incorrectly designate Annas, rather than
   Caiaphas, as the high priest during the ministry of Jesus and after his
   death.

3. In Acts 5:36–37 Luke has Paul's reputed teacher, Gamaliel, give in-
   correct dates for Theudas and blunder grossly by placing Judas the
   Galilean *after* Theudas.[22]

4. The notion of a worldwide famine in Acts 11:28 is contradicted by
   Acts itself, for in 11:29–30 we read that the congregation in Antioch
   was able to send aid to Jerusalem; only local famines took place during
   the period in question.[23]

Because Luke strings together occurrences in his gospel and in Acts by
means of loose chronological indications,[24] it could well be that his account
of Paul's life omitted some of its crucial elements and that he mistakenly connected unrelated events with his vague chronological references.[25]

Further, one should note the difference between the slightly more than four
chapters that Luke allots to the first thirteen to fourteen years of Paul's life as a
Christian[26] and the fourteen chapters[27] assigned to his last few years.[28]

Strictly speaking, Acts has no chronology nor does it show chronological
purpose in the occasional references to contemporary history. "In the second
part [of Acts], the only indications of time are those that are related to the
stories about Paul. They remain relative because there is no synchronization
with actual days from contemporary history."[29]

The "chronological" information offered by Luke is often conditioned by his
theological intentions; indeed it is widely recognized that Luke is keen to paint
Christianity as a politically safe movement[30] that has proved the validity of its
title and is ready to be adopted as a world religion. Acts 26:26 clearly illustrates
the universal claim for Christianity's renown when the apostle "Paul" says to
the Roman procurator Festus: "This was not done in the corner."[31]

Last but not least, an organization of the collection in Macedonia and
Achaia seems to suggest that Paul's mission in these provinces antedated the

Jerusalem conference. It would be strange indeed if at the Jerusalem conference Paul had promised to raise money from communities that did not yet exist.

THE NEW CHRONOLOGY

The above several objections reveal the dubious nature of the conventional harmonization of Acts with the letters. Historical investigation increasingly shows that we have been too uncritical with respect to Luke's chronological references. Therefore it is necessary to adopt a method for the establishment of Paul's chronology that proceeds solely on the basis of the letters and only afterwards attempts a critical evaluation of Acts. On this point I am indebted to Ferdinand Christian Baur (1792–1860) and especially to the American scholar John Knox (1900–1990), both of whom acknowledge the great superiority of the apostle's own letters over Luke's tendentious storytelling as a source for Paul's career. In 1845 F. C. Baur wrote:

> It would appear natural to suppose that in all the cases where the account in Acts do not altogether agree with statements of the Apostle, the latter must have such a decided claim to be considered authentic truth that the contradictions would hardly be worth attention. . . . The comparison of these two sources leads us to the conclusion that, considering the great differences between the two statements, historical truth must be entirely on one side or entirely on the other. . . . For the history of the Apostolic Age the Pauline Epistles must in any case take precedence over all the other New Testament writings as an authentic source.[32]

John Knox holds that the barest hint in the Pauline epistles is worth more than the most explicit statement in Acts. For

> a fact only suggested in the letters has a status which even the most unequivocal statement of Acts, if not otherwise supported, cannot confer. We may, with proper caution, use Acts to supplement the autobiographical data of the letters, but never to correct them.[33]

The revolutionary significance of John Knox' work for the chronology of Paul is this: By using Paul's letters as primary sources he is able not only to place Paul's mission in Greece before the Jerusalem conference, but also to date it a full decade earlier than generally supposed.

A RECONSTRUCTION OF THE CHRONOLOGY OF PAUL

One of the keystones of research on Paul is that the available sources establish beyond cavil three visits to Jerusalem by him as a Christian. Scholars speak of

the Cephas visit (Gal 1:18)
the conference visit (Gal 2:1)
the collection visit (Rom 15:25)

In Gal 1:15–24 Paul gives his solemn oath (v. 20) that he was in Jerusalem only once (v. 18) between the time of his conversion (vv. 15–16) and his attendance at the Jerusalem conference (2:1–10).

Taken together, the reported unanimity concerning the collection (Gal 2:10) and the history of the collection recorded in the letters gives powerful support to the contention that subsequent to the conference Paul returned to Jerusalem only on the occasion when he brought the collection.

Yet recently various scholars have objected to the view that Paul cannot have visited Jerusalem between his conversion and the conference. In order to substantiate their claim they have adduced autobiographical literature of antiquity in which persuasion rather than truth is the overriding concern.[34]

But what may be true of autobiographical literature in general cannot legitimately be held to obtain in a specific case, and especially one like that of Paul's letter to the Galatians. Facing stiff opposition from within the Galatian communities, Paul had no other choice than to be precise, the more so since in Gal 1:20 he swears to be telling the truth throughout his epistle.[35] Moreover, his adversaries who had invaded the Galatian churches *did* know how often Paul had been in Jerusalem and would surely have told the members of the congregations if he had left out a journey.[36]

Thus an additional journey to Jerusalem between his visit to Cephas and his participation in the Jerusalem conference fourteen years later must be excluded.[37]

The same is true for the time between the conference and Paul's final journey to Jerusalem; for once he began gathering the collection, any suspension or delay would be fatal to the project. Rather, the gathering came *directly* after the agreement over the collection and was not a long-postponed operation, planned before Paul's founding of his communities and only now, several years later, being implemented. In other words, a likelihood bordering on certainty indicates that Paul went to Jerusalem only three times, whereas in Acts we find him making no fewer than five such journeys.[38]

A reconstruction of the chronology of Paul must therefore begin with an analysis of Gal 1:6–2:10, the central pillar of any sustainable chronology of Paul's activity. For the sake of clarity I have divided the analysis of the long section running from Gal 1:6–2:10 into several parts, beginning with 1:6–10.

GALATIANS 1:6–10

> [6]I am astonished that you are so quickly deserting the one who called you by the grace of Christ and are turning to a different gospel—[7]which is really no gospel at all. Evidently some people are throwing you into confusion and are trying to pervert the gospel of Christ. [8]But even

1:6 *Christ* 1:7, 10, 12; 2:4. *Gospel* 1:7–9, 11; 2:2, 5, 7.

if we or an angel from heaven should proclaim a gospel other than what we proclaimed to you, let that one be accursed.

⁹As we have already said, so now I say again:

If anybody is proclaiming to you a gospel other than what you received, let that one be accursed.

¹⁰Am I now trying to win the approval of people, or of God?

Or am I trying to please people?

If I were still trying to please people, I would not be Christ's slave.

This section refers to an anti-Pauline agitation in Galatia. Some "troublemakers" have proclaimed to the Galatians a gospel contradictory to that of Paul, who considers their acceptance of this preaching no less than apostasy. At vv. 8–9 he twice hurls a curse at anyone who preaches contrary to his gospel. This curse, together with the blessing of peace and mercy bestowed in Gal 6:15 on faithful believers, employs antithesis to form a frame or *inclusio* for the epistle. In Gal 1:10 Paul poses two rhetorical questions and offers a truncated syllogism to demonstrate his probity and undermine charges of hypocrisy we may inferentially attribute to his opponents. It also forms a kind of transition to the next section: note that v. 11 begins with "for" (in the Greek, *gar*).

To be sure, Paul did not explicitly say that the opponents had attacked him directly. However, that is surely the implication of what Paul writes here and later specifies in condemning their demands for circumcision[39] and the retention of Jewish holidays and observances.[40]

To counter his opponents' claim that he was dependent on Jerusalem, Paul must be both precise and authoritative. He underscores his independence by an oath (v. 20) and the obvious importance of this issue allows us to find a solid basis for our reconstruction in Paul's statements:

GALATIANS 1:11–24

¹¹For I would have you know, brothers, that the gospel proclaimed by me is not of human origin.

¹²For I did not receive it from a human source, nor was I taught it, but it came through a revelation of Jesus Christ.

¹³For you have heard of my former life in Judaism, how I persecuted the church of God violently and tried to destroy it;

1:8 *Proclaim* 1:9, 11, 16, 23; *Let that one be accursed* 1:9.
1:10 *God* 1:13, 20, 24; 2:6.
1:12 *Revelation, reveal* 1:16; 2:2. *Jesus* 2:4.
1:13 *Judaism* 1:14. *Persecute* 1:23. *Destroy* 1:23.

[14]and I advanced in Judaism beyond many of my own age among
my people,
so extremely zealous was I for the traditions of my fathers.
　　[15]But when he who had set me apart from birth, and had called
me through his grace, [16]chose to reveal his Son to [or "in"] me so
that I might proclaim him among the Gentiles, I did not confer
with flesh and blood, [17]nor did I go up to Jerusalem to those who
were apostles before me; but I went away into Arabia and again
returned to Damascus.
　　[18]Then after three years I went up to Jerusalem to get to know
Cephas, and remained with him fifteen days. [19]But I saw none of
the other apostles except James, the Lord's brother.
　　[20]In what I am writing to you, before God, I do not lie.
　　[21]Then I went into the regions of Syria and Cilicia.
　　[22]And I was (still) unknown by face to the Christian churches in
Judea; [23]they only heard it said,
　　He who once persecuted us
　　is now proclaiming the faith
　　he once tried to destroy.

[24]And they praised God for me.

1:11–12 These verses, while echoing vv. 1–2, are intended to provide an authoritative certification for what follows: Paul's assertion of his genuine and
independent apostleship.
　　1:13–14 Paul adduces his audience's knowledge of his pre-Christian life
and emphasizes his former zeal for the law—a quality that not only caused
him to excel of his contemporaries, but also drove him to persecute the
church.[41]
　　1:15–16 Here Paul refers to his conversion experience; understanding it to
have involved a divine calling, he felt no need to obtain human sanction.
　　1:17 Accordingly, he says, he did not go to Jerusalem to confer with the first
apostles, and thereby he excludes any dependence on them. Paul's statement
that following this event he went to Arabia and again returned to Damascus
allows us no choice but to infer that at the time of his conversion he was in
Damascus[42] and that the persecution referred to in v. 13 took place in that
Syrian metropolis.[43]
　　In this verse Paul tells us that shortly after the conversion he spent some
time in Arabia, but since he gives no details about his stay, its purpose and du-
ration are unknown. Still, two assumptions may safely be made: *First*, the ac-

1:17 *Jerusalem* 1:18; 2:1.
1:18 *Cephas* 2:9a.

tion of the Nabataean ethnarch—an administrator serving under King Aretas IV and referred to in 2 Cor 11:32–33—was connected with Paul's stay in Arabia, for Arabia included the Nabataean territory. *Second*, Paul engaged in a mission among the Arab Nabataeans, who "appeared to be the 'closest kinsfolk' of the Jews who were still Gentiles,"[44] and this made him dangerous in the eyes of the Nabataean authorities.

This scenario is reflected in Paul's own testimony:

> [32]At Damascus, the ethnarch of King Aretas guarded the city of Damascus in order to seize me, [33]but I was let down in a basket through a window in the wall, and escaped his hands. (2 Cor 11:32–33)

The conclusions and assumptions noted above are corroborated by Paul's report of the need to escape from Damascus, for that necessity is due to pressure from the ethnarch of King Aretas IV, who held power from 9 BCE to 39 CE. This ethnarch was not a governor, but the headman of the Nabataeans, an ethnic group in the city of Damascus. Robert Jewett notwithstanding,[45] the action delineated cannot be connected with a political rule of the Nabataeans over Damascus between 37 and 39 CE, for that control never existed.[46] "The only information 2 Cor 11:32–33 provides us is that Paul must have fled from Damascus before the death of Aretas."[47]

Just how long he remained in Damascus after his conversion is uncertain, but to recover from the emotional trauma of such a conversion and become familiar with the essentials of Christian faith and teachings—to say nothing of gaining the trust of the community there—must have required at least six months. A mission to Nabataea, probably in company with Damascene colleagues, may well have lasted a year; and upon his return he likely preached to the Nabataean population in Damascus for another six months until the ethnarch sought his arrest. No doubt, as he found later in his career, preaching to those whom Jews regarded as Gentiles led to resistance from both groups. The time between Paul's conversion in Damascus and his first Jerusalem visit was thus probably a little more than two years, and thus less than the three years he reports in v. 18, because in antiquity fractional parts of the first and last years were counted as full years.

1:18–19 Here Paul recounts his first visit to Jerusalem as a Christian. His purpose was to get to know Cephas, and the visit lasted only fifteen days, during which time he saw none of the other apostles except for James, the Lord's brother.

1:20 Paul's gives his solemn oath to confirm the accuracy of his statements, and thus excludes the possibility of an additional visit between the first (related in v. 18) and the one mentioned in 2:1.

1:21–23 "Syria and Cilicia" in v. 21 identify the area to which Paul journeyed after his first visit to Jerusalem.[48] Refuting his opponents' arguments,

Paul stresses the fact that he left not only the immediate vicinity of Jerusalem, but its environs as well, for he was still "unknown by face to the Christian churches in Judea" (1:22). That "makes it unlikely that Jerusalem had been the scene of his activity as a persecutor."[49] What mattered was "that he left Judea after his two-week visit; there was no occasion whatever for a description of all his subsequent activities."[50] When Paul again mentions his dealings with the members of the Jerusalem congregation, he says nothing of where he had been during the "fourteen silent years," but describes only his negotiations in Jerusalem.

GALATIANS 2:1–10

[1]Then after fourteen years I went up again to Jerusalem with Barnabas and took Titus along with me. [2]I went up as the result of a revelation; and I laid before them—but privately before those who were of repute—the gospel that I preach among the Gentiles, lest somehow I should be running or had run in vain. [3]Yet even Titus, who was with me, a Greek, was not forced to be circumcised.

[4]But because of false brothers secretly brought in, who slipped in to spy out our freedom which we have in Christ Jesus, that they might bring us into bondage—[5]to them we did not yield submission even for a moment, that the truth of the gospel might be preserved for you.

[6]And from those who were reputed to be something—what they were makes no difference to me; God shows no partiality—those, I say, who were of repute added nothing to me;

[7]but on the contrary, when they saw that

I had been entrusted with the gospel to the Gentiles,
just as Peter had been entrusted with that to the circumcised

—[8]for he who worked through Peter for the apostleship for the circumcised
worked through me also for the Gentiles—

[9a]and when they perceived the grace that was given to me, James and Cephas and John, who were reputed to be the pillars, gave to me and Barnabas the right hand of fellowship, [agreeing] that

[9b]we should go to the Gentiles
and they to the circumcised;

2:1 *Titus* 2:3. *Barnabas* 2:9a.
2:2 *Repute* 2:6, 9a.
2:3 *Gentiles* 2:7–8, 9b. Circumcised 2:7–8, 9b.

[10]only they would have us remember the poor, which very thing I made every effort to do.

This passage gives a brief report of the *Jerusalem conference* that took place "fourteen years" (actually thirteen years) after the first visit related in v. 18. Responding to a revelation, Paul says, he traveled to Jerusalem along with Barnabas but also took Titus with him (vv. 1–2). An analysis of the agreement of the conference as reflected in v. 9 will help to make clear the real purpose of this meeting.

The agreement arrived at (v. 9b) established an ethnic division of the world missions in order to eliminate problems that arose from the commingling of Jewish and Gentile Christians. Paul has tacitly disavowed a mission to the Jews, since all his letters are directed to Gentiles, and Titus is the perfect representative of Paul's Gentile mission and the best possible evidence for Paul's statement in v. 6 that "those who were of repute added nothing to me."[51]

EVENTS OF THE JERUSALEM CONFERENCE

The primary issue at the Jerusalem Conference was whether Gentile Christians must be circumcised to become members of the Christian community.[52] Obviously this reflected an existing practice of accepting Gentiles into the community without circumcision and, further, reflects the activities of those whom Paul calls "false brothers," traditional Jews who had infiltrated the Antioch community in order "to spy out" the liberal practices of the Christians there.[53]

Outraged by this interference, Paul goes up to Jerusalem with Barnabas, and as an act of provocation takes with him the Gentile Christian Titus in an attempt to gain the assent of the Jerusalem leaders and community to what has been his own practice.

In Paul's description in Galatians we can distinguish two separate sets of negotiations: the one in Gal 2:2a takes place within the framework of an assembly of the congregation; the other, detailed by Gal 2:2b, 6–10, concerns Paul's pact with a small group of community leaders whom Paul ironically designates as "the pillars": Cephas, James, and John. The chronological relationship between the discussions is not clear.

After what must have been hard bargaining and heated arguments, Paul was able to wring from "the pillars" an agreement that the Gentile Christians need not be circumcised. At any rate, Paul's Greek companion Titus was not forced to be circumcised.[54] Nevertheless, the agreement was probably not an entirely amicable one; indeed, it must be assumed that at least initially the "false brothers" had considerable support in the Jerusalem community for their demand that Titus be circumcised.[55] And "the pillars" probably remained at least partly on their side.

In spite of this, the Jerusalem community had assented to his mission to the Gentiles without the requirement of circumcision, and the solemn handshake that sealed their agreement signified both their equality and the mission's *success*. To this the Jerusalem Christians could not close their eyes. No doubt the readiness of Paul and Barnabas to commit the Gentile Christian communities to a gift of money carried a good deal of weight.

Scholars have puzzled a great deal over this collection.[56] Some have understood it as analogous to the temple tax that every male Jew had to pay annually,[57] while others point out that with it the promise of the pilgrimage of the nations is fulfilled.[58] Still others claim that the Jerusalem leaders had insisted on a collection to be gathered from the Pauline communities, which would thereby adopt the traditional status of "god-fearers."[59]

Be that as it may, in v. 10 Paul mentions only one qualification made by "the pillars" when they accepted the divided mission (v. 9): Their single condition was that "we remember the poor, which very thing I made every effort to do" (v. 10). In the agreement, both the representatives of the Gentile Christians committed themselves to remember the poor. This is apparent from the first person plural in v. 10a, though v. 10b mentions only Paul's zeal in fulfilling this obligation.

One further difference between v. 10a and v. 10b should be noted: the verb in v. 10a appears in the present subjunctive, whereas v. 10b uses the first aorist. In this context the present tense of the verb "to remember"[60] expresses a new action of Paul and Barnabas, not the continuation of an old one. Indeed, "If the reference were simply to a continuance of almsgiving one wonders why the matter should have been included in the agenda of the council."[61]

Thus at the conference in Jerusalem it was agreed that the Gentile Christian congregations would undertake the responsibility of providing financial support for the poor at Jerusalem. Note that Gal 2:10 (". . . *we* remember the poor . . . *I* made every effort to do") suggests that Paul eagerly assumed the obligation to collect funds from his communities. "Therefore the most important resolution of the conference was the least apparent: the collection for the Jerusalem community; and Paul's further efforts for this collection were among the most important of his activity."[62]

THE COLLECTION AS CRITERION

We are now ready to turn to the collection as an external criterion for establishing a chronological framework. As we have seen, it was shortly *after* the conference that Paul began an operation intended to provide support for the congregation in Jerusalem. The remark "which very thing I made every effort to do" in the second half of the verse further indicates that the collection was known to the Galatians and that it was still underway.

And not only does Paul speak of his zeal for the collection as if that fervor was known to the Galatians, but they also knew from Galatians 1–2 about

Paul's persecution of Christians (1:13); the divided mission indicated by "James, Cephas, John to the Jews, Paul and Barnabas to the Gentiles" (2:9); and that the collection had not yet been completed.

Can one exegetically extend these results in the light of the information in 1 Cor 16:1 that Paul had instructed the Galatians about the manner for gathering the collection? Before attempting to answer this question, let us first examine a thesis of Dieter Georgi that would deny the validity of this question. After emphasizing that "it was precisely in Galatia that he [Paul] began to organize the collection again"[63] Georgi points out:

> The call for a collection, mentioned in I Cor. 16:1, occurs after the composition and delivery of the Epistle to the Galatians. It must have been conveyed to the Galatians by different means. According to I Cor. 16:1, Paul had also asked the Corinthians to participate in the collection after giving similar instructions to the Galatians.[64]

To be sure, Galatians says nothing about the organization of the collection; but the gathering of such a fund is clearly adduced in Gal 2:10b, and Paul's zeal for it is both stated here and presumably known to the Galatians. Thus it appears that the collection was fully under way in the Galatian communities before the troublemaking opponents arrived. Georgi, however, denies both the organization of the collection and Paul's zeal in carrying it out at the time of composition of Galatians.

Concerning the *organization* of the collection, Georgi writes,

> Yet, nothing at all is said about a collection being organized, or to be organized, in these congregations—not even when he reports on the collection at the Jerusalem summit. Indeed, had a collection been started in those Galatian congregations, Paul would at least have referred to it by writing something like, "As you know . . ."[65]

This begs the question. If the collection in Galatia had already been in operation before the letter, the mention of Paul's zeal would have been enough for everyone to understand his reference.

By way of denying Paul's zeal for carrying out the collection at the time when he was writing Galatians, Georgi asserts that when Paul says "which very thing I made every effort to do," he

> refers only to his zealous efforts undertaken to see the second point of the agreement fulfilled after the convention had come to an end.[66]

According to this view, Paul began the collection with zeal directly after the conference, but when the Antioch incident[67]—the withdrawal of the Jewish Christians in Antioch from the table-fellowship with Gentile Christians upon the demand of Jesus' brother James—"disrupted the bond of trust previously revived at Jerusalem,"[68] the collection effort came to a standstill. Later, Georgi proposes, Paul reinstituted the collection in his independent mission after he had won back the Galatians, and the first evidence of this renewal is 1 Cor 16:1.[69]

Four observations speak against this view:

1. Georgi's assumption that Paul was able to win back the Galatians through his letter is problematical. If Paul had been unsuccessful—a distinct possibility in light of the content of the letter—then Galatians would have been written *after* 1 Corinthians. Otherwise, the reference to the Galatians in the section about the collection (1 Cor 16:1) would not be understandable, for this reference strongly implies that the relationship between the Galatian congregations and Paul is intact. Surely if Galatians was written before 1 Corinthians and the Galatians had subsequently broken away from Paul, he could hardly instruct the Corinthians to gather the collection as he had instructed the Galatians to do!

2. The noticeable parallelism between Galatians and Romans in the sections that deal with justification[70] strongly suggests that Galatians was written shortly before Romans.

3. Similarities in style and language link Galatians and 2 Corinthians. The most important are the following:

Language and structure: Gal 1:6–9/2 Cor 11:4–5
Several specifics: Damascus, oath, fourteen years (Gal 1:17–22/2 Cor 11–12:4)
Terms: false brothers[71] (Gal 2:4/2 Cor 11:26)
    to bring into bondage[72] (Gal 2:4/2 Cor 11:20)
    to consume[73] (Gal 5:15/2 Cor 11:20)
    angel[74] (Gal 1:8; 4:14/2 Cor 11:14; 12:7)

According to Udo Borse, these findings "make sense only if the statements of the one letter were still alive in the thoughts of the apostle as he dictated the other, so that he was able to repeat these statements in the later writing in a varied but nevertheless surprisingly similar manner."[75]

4. In Rom 15:26 Paul reports that "Macedonia and Achaia have been pleased[76] to share their resources with the poor among the saints at Jerusalem." If the collection in Galatia is supposed to have been undertaken along with the collection in Achaia (Corinth) and Macedonia (Philippi, Thessalonica), why does Paul fail to mention Galatia here? Or had the collection from Galatia already been delivered? But if this were the case, it is surprising that the Galatian collection is not at least mentioned in 2 Corinthians 8–9, a section that specifically deals with the collection and that was composed before Rom 15:26. Therefore it seems highly probable that Paul was not able to report a contribution from the Galatians, and that would seem to indicate that the collection in Galatia had fallen through.

If the absence of a reference to the collection from Galatia in Rom 15:26 and 2 Corinthians 8–9 offers a valid argument from silence, then those who defend the chronological priority of Galatians over 1 Corinthians must explain how Paul is able to refer in 1 Cor 16:1 to a suspended collection in Galatia.

The question raised at the beginning about the relationship of 1 Cor 16:1 to Gal 2:10 and about the antecedent history of the collection in Galatia should therefore be answered as follows: Gal 2:10 and 1 Cor 16:1 look back on a collection in Galatia that had proceeded beyond the initial stage. The text of 1 Cor 16:1–2 reiterates detailed instructions about the manner of gathering the collection and thus clearly indicates that such measures had been agreed upon. The zeal for the collection that Paul declares in Gal 2:10 is likewise understandable only if the collection in Galatia had already made some progress—and such an understanding fits in well with 1 Cor 16:1; but thereafter we do not hear anything more about the collection in Galatia. Because it is not mentioned in Rom 15:26 and 2 Corinthians 8–9, we have good reason to conclude that the Galatian collection was halted as a result of the opposition to Paul mounted by the "false brothers" (2:4).

THE COLLECTION IN I AND 2 CORINTHIANS AND IN ROMANS
For the present, let us see what we can learn about the collection from 1 and 2 Corinthians and Romans, the only letters besides Galatians that mention it.

The earliest reference to the collection, as discussed above, appears in 1 Cor 16:1–2 as a response to the addressees' question about *how* they should go about collecting the money. Since Paul told them to follow the example of the Galatian churches, their knowledge of the collection there is clearly presupposed.

Two remarks in 2 Corinthians indicate that the Macedonian and Achaian collections began around the same time.

> [8:1]We want you to know, brothers, about the grace of God granted to the churches of *Macedonia*; [2]for in a severe test of affliction, their abundance of joy and their extreme poverty have overflowed in a wealth of generosity on their part. [3]For, as I can testify, they voluntarily gave according to their means, and even beyond their means, [4]begging us urgently for the grace of taking part in this ministry to the saints. (2 Cor 8:1–4)

> I know your willingness, of which I boast about you to the people of Macedonia, saying that *Achaia* has been ready since last year; and your zeal has stirred up most of them. (2 Cor 9:2)

Historical References
The Passover allusions in 1 Cor 5:7–8 strongly suggest that Paul wrote 1 Corinthians in the spring. In view of references to the past[77] and the time

necessary to organize the collection from Ephesus, where 1 Corinthians was written,[78] Paul probably spent at least one winter in Ephesus.

Galatians 4:13 ("You know that it was because of an illness that I preached the gospel to you the first time") and the reference to the Galatian churches in 1 Cor 16:1 render it probable that after the Jerusalem conference Paul undertook a second visit to Galatia, in order to organize the collection there. After that he traveled to Ephesus[79] and used that city as a base for his collection project in the churches of Macedonia and Achaia.[80]

Initial Mission in Macedonia and Achaia

When taken together, Paul's remark that "Some are arrogant, as though I were not coming to you"[81] and his reference to a prior letter to the Corinthians, "I wrote you in my previous letter not to associate with fornicators,"[82] make it highly probable that when Paul composed 1 Corinthians, he had not been in Corinth for quite some time. Other passages also hint that the founding of the Corinthian congregation had not occurred in the recent past:

Apollos' stay in Corinth[83] after Paul had left the city, and his later presence in Ephesus with Paul.[84]

The multiple problems that had arisen in Corinth: cf. especially the numerous questions that Paul had to answer in 1 Corinthians 7.

Paul's detailed knowledge of the many spiritual gifts and practices in the Corinthian congregation.[85]

The fact that "many"[86] had died since Paul's last visit.[87]

The announcement of Paul's *sudden* arrival[88] and reasons proffered for the delay.

Paul's reference to having fought with beasts in Ephesus in the past[89]—a peril he must have survived—suggests an extended stay in Ephesus where 1 Corinthians was composed, and an even longer absence from Corinth.

Thus Paul's stay in Ephesus at the time of the composition of 1 Corinthians 16 followed the founding visit in Corinth by a considerable period of time. And the greater the chronological separation of the two, the more likely it is that between his founding of the Corinthian community and his writing of 1 Corinthian in Ephesus, Paul had been traveling elsewhere and thus could have participated in the Jerusalem conference.

Besides, "a few commentators have noticed the nature of the Corinthians' question concerning the collection for the saints implies that they had been informed of this project only shortly before."[90] Therefore its institution cannot have happened at the founding visit. Against this point it might be argued that Paul omitted any mention of the collection during the first visit for tactical reasons: he feared alienating the new congregation. But this objection does not hold water, because a later institution of the collection could not help but produce much the same effect and, owing to the apostle's absence, would likely have raised suspicions and lowered contributions. Thus the lack of evidence that the collection was mentioned during the founding visit in Corinth speaks for dating that visit before the Jerusalem conference also.

PHIL 4:15–16: A REFERENCE TO THE BEGINNING OF PAUL'S MISSION IN EUROPE

[15]You Philippians yourselves know that in the beginning of the gospel [*en archê tou euaggeliou*], when I left Macedonia, no church shared with me in giving and receiving except you only; [16]for even when I was in Thessalonica you sent me help more than once. (Phil 4:15–16)

This passage not only specifies the time lapse between 1 Corinthians and the founding of the congregations in Macedonia and Achaia, but it also suggests the chronological setting of the mission in Europe. Here Paul speaks of the "early days of my mission"[91] as following upon and including his mission in Macedonia. This phrase is most naturally understood as an indication of the beginning of Paul's missionary activity as a whole,[92] though this does not fit in with the standard view that Paul preached in Greece only after the conference. 1 Thess 2:2 and 3:1, 6 then indicate the cities along the route of Paul's initial mission to Europe: Philippi, Thessalonica, Athens, and Corinth.

In this passage the term "gospel" designates an action[93] and is best translated as "proclamation of the gospel."[94] The noun "beginning"[95] does not have the technical sense it assumed two generations later in the Lukan and Johannine writings, where it indicates the very beginning of the church.[96] Here it indicates simply the *early* period of the Christian movement.

Since in this letter Paul speaks primarily from his own perspective and not that of the Philippians, *en archê tou euaggeliou* is best translated as "in the beginning of my proclamation of the gospel," for Paul views his mission in Greece, which began in Macedonia, as the initial period of his evangelistic activity.[97]

Since it is certain that Paul was active as a missionary before the conference, that he engaged in a Gentile mission independent of Antioch (remember Titus!), and that he could hardly have designated as the beginning of his missionary activity an effort that began seventeen years after his conversion, then it must be that Paul had evangelized in Greece before the Jerusalem conference, and this must have occurred sometime in the thirteen years before the conference that Paul briefly mentions in Gal 2:1 but does not further explain.

In view of Paul's approximate understanding of *archê*, it is quite possible that he reckoned his presumed activity in Arabia, Damascus, and Syria/Cilicia as the early phase of his proclamation of the gospel. Since Christian communities probably existed in these localities at a very early date, and since he elsewhere expresses an unwillingness to preach "where Christ had already been introduced, lest I build on someone else's foundation,"[98] it is understandable that Paul would leave the eastern shore of the Mediterranean soon after his conversion and extend his mission to Greece. Here he was able to lay a foundation of his own making[99] and allow others to cultivate or plant on the ground he had prepared: note that he allowed Apollos to water his garden.[100]

Therefore, if Paul's Macedonian mission that included Philippi can be understood as an early stage of his evangelistic activity, then 1 Thessalonians surely derives from that first phase of the outreach to Europe. And inasmuch as the absence of a reference to the collection in 1 Thessalonians strongly implies that this letter was not composed while Paul was engaged in satisfying the second part of the Jerusalem agreement, this early dating of his mission to Thessalonica becomes even more certain. For one thing, Phil 4:16 indicates that a mission in Thessalonica was connected with the initial period of proclamation; for another, in 1 Thessalonians Paul looks back to the founding of the congregation. One need note only 1:9–10, a summary of Paul's missionary proclamation in Thessalonica, and 2:1, where he recalls the acceptance he encountered in that Macedonian city.

Furthermore, Paul's reference to support from the Philippian congregation[101] accords well with his statements about working day and night in Thessalonica[102] and supporting himself in Corinth.[103]

The first letter to the Thessalonians provides us with much information about the route Paul took during his founding mission in Greece: the apostle traveled from Philippi to Athens, sent Timothy from there to Thessalonica, and met his assistant again at Corinth, where 1 Thessalonians was composed. And one may reasonably presume that 1 Thessalonians was composed shortly after the founding of the Corinthian community. Thus our view is confirmed that the founding visit to Corinth did not occur during the period when the collection was being organized, but rather before the Jerusalem conference.

The combination of all these facts renders it highly probable that Paul operated a mission in Greece *before* the Jerusalem conference and for precisely that reason was able to promise "the pillars" that he would raise money from these communities for the church in Jerusalem.

I THESS 4:13–17 AND I COR 15:51–52: EXTERNAL CRITERIA OF PAUL'S EARLY MACEDONIAN MISSION[104]

We can begin with the insight that the earliest beginnings of Christianity were characterized by an apocalyptic tenor and dominated by an ardent expectation of the end of the present era. Though Jesus' own beliefs in this matter may be debatable,[105] there is absolutely no doubt about the imminent expectation of the first Christian generation.

Nevertheless, *internal* criteria such as changes of thought and/or theological developments cannot be adduced in making chronological judgments; nor are the concepts of "apocalyptic" and "imminent expectation," and the related notion of the "kingdom of God," sufficiently explicit to serve as *external* criteria for an "early dating" of 1 Thessalonians.

The question then arises whether one may more closely delineate the concept of imminent expectation so that it may serve chronological purposes. More specifically, we are concerned with two questions: whether early Christians offered specific predictions as to the arrival of the end and, even more crucial, whether any such forecasts can be found in Paul's writings.

Should these questions be answered in the affirmative, we would have one or more *external* points of reference for determining the order and approximate date of texts and letters based on their statements concerning when the end is to be expected.

The imminent expectation of primitive Christianity can be delineated precisely enough to enable us to say that the Christians of the first generation after the death and "resurrection" of Jesus generally thought they would no longer have to face death, for the arrival of the Lord, or the kingdom of God, was immediately at hand.

We find this belief in 1 Thess 4:13–17, where Paul does not reckon with any more deaths until the second coming. Yet, according to 1 Cor 15:51–52 the majority will die and only a minority survive. This is evident from Paul's formulation in v. 51b: "We shall not all sleep, but we shall all be changed." The emphasis in this prophetic declaration is clearly that *all* will be transformed, the dead as well as the living. This statement assumes that a quantitative change has occurred in the proportions of the (still) living and the (in the meantime) dead in Paul's circles and thus also in Corinth. This change effected the shift in Paul's formulation. Now "the present generation of Christians can retain only the certainty that not all of them will fall among the group of *nekroi*."[106] The wording of 1 Cor 15:51b thus leads to the view that most will die before the parousia.

The consequence for the chronological question is that 1 Thessalonians can reasonably be dated to the late thirties and 1 Corinthians to the early fifties of the first century.

Helmut Koester offers a dubious objection to this methodology in *A Colloquy on New Testament Studies*.[107] His argument runs thus:

> As you move closer to the parousia, that is, the later it is in time, the fewer [Christians] . . . you would expect to die. So you could just turn [Lüdemann's argument] around and come to the opposite result. . . . Ten years before the parousia you would expect that quite a few will die, but one day before the parousia you would expect that everybody [among Christians] would still be alive.

My response is as follows: While it is true that apocalyptic thinkers more or less expect the end to happen within their own lifetimes,[108] they seldom offer dates or numbers of years; as a result, their statements should not and cannot

not be used for chronological purposes. But the case is different with Paul, for two passages of his letters not only contain specific dates, but also have a genetic connection with each other. Therefore, my method is valid for the first generation of Christians because of the specific nature of these texts.

John Knox, who accepts just such a use of these two passages, 1 Thess 4:13–17 and 1 Cor 15:51–52, for an early dating of Paul's earliest letter, expresses his concurrence as follows:

> Gerd Lüdemann calls attention to a very telling piece of external evidence which all but requires an early date for 1 Thessalonians— more particularly, its priority to 1 Corinthians. This is the fact that 1 Thess 4:13–18 clearly reflects a period in the church's history when very few Christians had died. Lüdemann points out that in the very beginning the Lord's return was confidently expected within a few months or at most years. The first Christian evangelists did not deal, and had no occasion to deal, with the tender problem created by the death of a believer before the Parousia. Would such a one witness and share in the glory of it? No one had need to ask. But this situation could not have lasted long. Yet, it was apparently still substantially unchanged when Paul first preached the gospel of the Lord's return to the Thessalonians. Lüdemann has no difficulty [in] showing that the eschatological teaching of 1 Corinthians (esp. 15:51–52) reflects a different, and later, objective situation. I must say, therefore, that for me at least the weightiest evidence for regarding 1 Thessalonians as Paul's earliest extant letter is external.[109]

Knox adds another argument in favor of an early date of 1 Thessalonians:

> I cannot help pointing to a wider implication in Paul's silence at Thessalonica about the faithful dead than that with which Lüdemann is most concerned. May we not find here a very telling refutation of the traditional and prevailing chronology of Paul's career with its initial "silent years"? Paul has evidently reached Macedonia before any Christians—certainly before more than a few Christians—have died. Indeed, this consideration, if it stood alone, would suggest an even earlier date of his European mission than other data (particularly the "after three years" of Gal 1:18) allow us to propose.[110]

Let me hasten to add that Paul's missionary policy "to preach the gospel not where Christ had already been named"[111] confirms an early date of Paul's European mission. Members of the early Christian movement would in all likelihood have arrived in the Roman provinces of Macedonia and Achaia before 50 CE, the traditional date of Paul's European mission, with the result that

Paul would not have been able to follow his missionary policy. Establishing the strong possibility of an early date for this mission renders it more probable that Paul may indeed have reached Macedonia before other Christian preachers, and was thus able to formulate and carry out a missionary policy based on priority.

PAUL'S MISSION IN CORINTH (ACTS 18:1–17): A MODEL EXEGESIS

Critical scholars agree that the anonymous author of Luke-Acts was not an eyewitness of what he reported, but rather composed an apologetic history of early Christianity on the basis of what he gleaned from oral and written sources. The editorial features of his work are clearly discernible. Yet occasionally Paul's letters point to historical kernels in Luke's work that in turn serve to further secure the historical value of Paul's statements. This seems to be true for Luke's account of Paul's mission in Corinth.

The following section on Acts 18:1–17 is a *model exegesis* of how to gain reliable information from Acts on the basis of Paul's own statements in his letters. I have indicated by *italics* passages that derive from Luke's editorial hand. Keep in mind that not all sections in Acts allow us to gain dependable data from them.

ACTS 18:1–17

¹After this he left Athens and went to Corinth. ²There he found *a Jew called* Aquila, a native of Pontus, who had recently come from Italy with his wife Priscilla, because Claudius had issued an edict that *all* Jews should leave Rome. And he approached them, ³and, because he was of the same trade, he stayed with them, and they worked together, for by trade they were tentmakers.

⁴*And he argued in the synagogue every Sabbath, and sought to persuade Jews and Greeks.*

⁵When Silas and Timothy came down from Macedonia, Paul devoted himself entirely to proclaiming the word, *testifying to the Jews that the Messiah was Jesus.* ⁶*And when they opposed him and resorted to abuse, he shook out his garments and said to them, "Your blood be on your heads! I am innocent; from now on I shall go to the Gentiles."* ⁷*So he withdrew from there* and went to the house of a worshipper of God *named* Titius Justus, who lived next door to the synagogue. ⁸Crispus, the ruler of the synagogue, now became a

18:2 *Jew(s)* 18:4–5, 12, 14.
18:4 *Persuade* 18:13.
18:5 *Paul* 18:9, 12, 14. *Word* 18:11.
18:7 *God* 18:11, 13. *Worship* 18:13. *Synagogue* 18:8, 17.
18:8 *Ruler* 18:17.

believer in the Lord along with all his household; and many of the Corinthians listened and believed, and were baptized.

⁹*One night in a vision the Lord said to Paul, "Do not be afraid, but speak and do not be silent;* ¹⁰*for I am with you, and no one shall attempt to do you harm; for there are many in this city who are my people."*

¹¹So he stayed for a year and six months, *teaching the word of God among them.*

¹²*But when Gallio was proconsul of Achaia, the Jews made a concerted attack on Paul and brought him before the* tribunal, ¹³*saying,* "This man persuades people to worship God in ways that are against the law." ¹⁴*Paul was about to open his mouth, when Gallio said to the Jews, "If it had been a question of wrongdoing or vicious crime, I would not hesitate to listen to you Jews;* ¹⁵*but since it is a matter of questions about words and names and your own law, you may see to it yourselves; I have no mind to be a judge of these matters."* ¹⁶*And he drove them away from the* tribunal. ¹⁷*And they all seized Sosthenes, the ruler of the synagogue, and beat him in front of the* tribunal. *But Gallio paid no attention to this.*

STRUCTURE

> 1: From Athens to Corinth
> 2–3: Paul works together with Aquila and Priscilla
> 4: Paul argues every Sabbath in the synagogue
> 5–8: Arrival of Silas and Timothy from Macedonia leads to an intensified missionary work by Paul
> 9–10: The Lord speaks in a vision to Paul
> 11: Note of Paul's length of stay in Corinth (eighteen months) during which he taught the word of God
> 12–17: The Jews drag Paul before the tribunal of proconsul Gallio

LUKE'S PURPOSE

18:2–3 The word "all"[112] is clearly a hyperbolic generalization typical of Luke-Acts.[113] By the reference to the emperor Claudius, Luke attempts to join the history of salvation with profane history.[114] Note Luke's earlier reference to Claudius.[115]

18:4 This verse exemplifies Luke's motif of Paul's first addressing himself to the Jews, and in anticipation of the next unit, vv. 5–8, it identifies the two groups involved: Jews and Gentiles.

18:12 *Gallio* 18:17. *Tribunal* 18:16–17.
18:13 *Law* 18:15.

18:5–8 Verse 5 describes in Lukan language Paul's intensified missionary activity. The content of the testimony that "the Messiah was Jesus" derives from Luke, being directed as in other passages[116] at the Jews. Typically, they resort to repudiation and charges of blasphemy, to which Paul responds in v. 6 with the symbolic action of shaking the dust off his clothes[117] and, having declared his innocence of any wrongdoing, breaks off all contact with them. By invoking the theme of blood-guilt, Luke's Paul echoes various passages from the Hebrew Bible;[118] he disavows any responsibility for the failure of his fellow Jews to accept Jesus as the Messiah; and in turning to Gentiles, Paul avoids repudiating his commission by repeating the course he followed in Pisidian Antioch.[119] Verses 7–8 then describe the success of the Gentile mission in Corinth.

18:9–10 "Vision" is a common Lukan narrative device[120] by means of which the assurance of the Lord (here = Christ) intensifies the drama of the scene. Furthermore, by foretelling that Paul will not undergo any harm in Corinth, the promise of the visionary Christ provides a transition to the subsequent episode before Gallio.

18:11 In Luke-Acts the term "word of God" signifies the content of the Christian preaching.[121]

18:12–17 The accusation in v. 13 that Paul "persuades people to worship God in ways that are against the law" refers to the Jewish law, not Roman statutes—as Gallio's answer in vv. 14–15 shows. Since during his last visit to Jerusalem Paul is confronted with similar Jewish charges,[122] the present accusation may be seen as a forerunner of the later theme. Historically, then, it does not belong here and therefore likely derives from Luke.

Indeed, the whole scene before Gallio is not even the mangled report of a trial, but clearly a literary presentation of a non-trial intended to show why such a proceeding is illegitimate. Even a cursory reading reveals the absence of any conversation between Paul and Gallio. The only exchange is between the Jews and Gallio, who by refusing to accept the Jewish charge shows himself unwilling to interfere in the controversy between Jews and Christians, and thus a model statesman.[123] For Luke, the vicarious beating of the ruler of the synagogue in v. 17 constitutes an ironic punishment of the Corinthian Jews for their attack on Paul and also provides a bit of dramatic relief, the more so since the beating goes unpunished.

TRADITIONS REWORKED BY LUKE
Before reconstructing the traditions that Luke reworked let me make a point that is all too commonly overlooked in studies of Acts. Though Luke often reports more than one visit by Paul to a given locality, only one account presents detailed information about the apostle's activity there, while any other visit is painted in broad strokes.[124] The following catalogue lists the detailed reports first, followed by those of a general nature:

Lystra: 14:8–20; cf. 14:21 and 16:1–3
Philippi: 16:12–40; cf. the two visits in 20:2, 3–6
Thessalonica: 17:1–10; cf. 20:2
Ephesus: 19:1–20:1; cf. 18:19–21

Luke's treatment of Corinth (18:1–17; cf. 20:2–3) follows this same pattern.

It is unlikely that local traditions to which Luke had access described only one *specific visit*. He seems rather to have gathered various reports relating Paul's several visits to a given locality and combined them into a single account. In 18:1–17 six elements of tradition can be identified:

Paul travels from Athens to Corinth. (v. 1)
In Corinth Paul meets Aquila and Priscilla—who as Jews had to leave because of the edict of Claudius and had recently[125] arrived in Corinth from Rome—and works with them. (vv. 2–3)
Silas and Timothy arrive from Macedonia. (v. 5a)
Paul intensifies his preaching of the gospel in Corinth. (vv. 5b–8)
Paul stays in Corinth for eighteen months. (v. 11)[126]
Incidents occur involving Gallio and Sosthenes. (vv. 12–17)

ABSOLUTE DATES

18:2 The date of the expulsion of the Jews from Rome is usually set in 49 CE.[127] The Roman biographer Suetonius (early second century CE) writes:

Claudius expelled the Jews from Rome who were exceedingly riotous because of the instigator Chrestus.[128] (*Lives of the Caesars. Claudius* 25[129])

The expulsion of the Jews by Claudius is also reported Acts 18:2. But the date 49 CE rests on the information supplied by the fifth-century priest Orosius:

Josephus reports that the Jews were expelled from the city [of Rome] by Claudius in his ninth year. I, however, am more convinced by Suetonius, who asserts as follows: Claudius expelled the Jews from Rome who were extremely riotous because of the instigator Chrestus. (*Historiae adversum paganos* 7.6.15[130])

The passage from Suetonius is accurately cited by Orosius. Yet, the indication of the year of the expulsion is dubious, for Josephus' works, which may have been preserved in their complete form, do not contain such a report. Besides, in view of the secondary character of Orosius' work and the questionable indication of this source, one can place little reliance on the expulsion date he has preserved.[131]

Besides, the contrast between Suetonius and Josephus does not fit. After writing that "Josephus" dates the expulsion of the Jews in the ninth year of

Claudius, Orosius would be expected to give Suetonius' dating—especially since he prefers it! But that is not the case. To be sure, Suetonius gives no dating at all and does not "claim that the emperor Claudius had expelled the Jews from Rome in the year 49 CE.[132] Orosius may have preferred Suetonius' report owing to apologetic reasons, for in his work he was trying to collect references to Christ by Gentile writers.

Furthermore, an attractive alternative thesis is that Orosius' source derived the date of the expulsion by subtracting the eighteen months found in v. 11 from the dates of Gallio's term in office—a tenure that could be determined from archival records.[133] Hence it is certainly secondary.[134]

In contrast, the Roman historian Dio Cassius reports an imperial command regarding the Jews for the year 41 CE. He writes:

> As for the Jews, who had again increased so greatly that by reason of their multitude it would have been hard without raising a tumult to bar them from the city, he did not drive them out (*exêlasen*), but ordered them, while continuing their traditional mode of life, not to hold meetings.[135] (*Roman History* 60.6.6)

The wording of the passage seems to indicate that Dio Cassius has relied on a tradition that was also available to Suetonius, but Dio Cassius has corrected it by denying that Claudius expelled (all) the Jews.[136]

It is worth noting that Suetonius' language can be interpreted to mean that only those Jews who rioted because of the instigator Chrestus were driven out. In this case Dio's statement offers no contradiction, since he denies only that there was a general expulsion like the one under Tiberius:

> As the Jews flocked to Rome in great numbers and were converting many of the natives to their ways, he [Tiberius] drove most of them out (*exêlasen*).[137] (*Roman History* 57.18.5a)

Moreover, the order not to hold cultic meetings amounted almost to the same as an expulsion but was probably not enforced.[138]

Only if one tries to combine Acts' statement about the expulsion of *all* the Jews from Rome with Suetonius' account does the date of the expulsion becomes problematic. Be that as it may, there was in all likelihood only *one* edict against the Jews, reported by Suetonius *and* Dio Cassius. "It would certainly be strange for one of them to mention only the latter edict, and the other, only the former."[139]

Irrespective of the question of whether Dio Cassius used Suetonius' report or is dependent with Suetonius on a common source (which is more probable), we have plenty of reason to assume that Dio purposely neglected to take over the name "Chrestus" from his source. He persistently ignored Christianity. "It is difficult to believe that his total silence about Christianity was not deliberate."[140] Therefore the lack of any reference to *Chrêstos* in Dio's work is not, as Joseph A. Fitzmyer opines, "a major obstacle to the identification" of the two anti-Jewish actions[141] narrated by Suetonius and Dio.

The historical kernel of these reports is no doubt the following: In 41 CE, Claudius issued a decree regarding the Jews; it pertained to the disturbances that had arisen in a synagogue and had involved Chrestus. The decree entailed the expulsion of those Jews who had been directly involved in the disturbances. One may, therefore, conclude that the tradition in Acts 18:2–3 could very well derive from Paul's first visit to Corinth around 41 CE, a date that nicely fits the chronology developed solely on the basis of the letters.

18:12–17 From the Gallio inscription we know that the proconsul held office in 51–52 CE.[142] With the date of the first visit in Corinth set by Paul's arrival from Athens (v. 1), it is readily apparent that Paul's second or third visit could well have occurred during Gallio's tenure.

PETER LAMPE AND THE "ACTS 18 CHRONOLOGY"

Peter Lampe's massive volume *From Paul to Valentinus* has been rightly hailed a masterful work on early Christianity in Rome. Unfortunately, its enthusiastic reception has also led to an uncritical use of Acts that turns back the clock in the area of Lukan research. In the course of analyzing Acts 18:1–11, Lampe introduces a new term—"Acts chronology"[143]—and on page 15 earnestly claims that the "Acts 18 chronology" is to be trusted more than that of the Roman historian Dio Cassius, "who edited his chronological information at the end of the second century at the earliest," while "the 'Acts 18 chronol-ogy' . . . is at least a century earlier."[144] Invoking no further evidence, Lampe concludes: "Even if the latter is burdened with uncertainties, a dating based on Dio's report is even more burdened."[145]

However, Lampe's dating totally ignores the redactional characteristics of Luke that argue against using his "chronology" uncritically. Moreover, Dio Cassius had archival material at his disposal and was a distinguished Roman historian. Besides, as was demonstrated above, Luke made many historical blunders. Worse yet, Acts 18 neither presents nor presupposes any chronology at all. Viewed as a whole, Luke-Acts simply lacks a chronology.

In addition, the "chronological" statements about the expulsion of "all" Jews from Rome, Paul's stay in Corinth for eighteen months, and Paul's trial before Gallio cannot be used to establish a critical sequence of events.

Consider also that "what one can read in many places, namely that the year 49 for the edict of Claudius fits exactly with the relative chronology of Acts, is precisely what could make Orosius' note suspicious."[146] The year 41 CE, *not* 49 CE, is therefore the most likely date for the edict of Claudius concerning the Jews, the more so since one would expect Josephus and Tacitus (whose reports about the first six years of Claudius have been lost) to make at least a passing reference to such an act.[147] It is indeed regrettable that Lampe shows so little awareness of the real problem of the Luke-Acts chronology, of the best way to determine both the most likely date of Claudius' edict against the Jews and that of Paul's first arrival in Corinth, and of a persuasive way to establish individual data concerning Paul's founding visit in Corinth.

PIECES OF TRADITION WITH HISTORICAL VALUE

18:1 Paul's trip from Athens to Corinth took place during his first missionary effort in Greece. This is clearly shown by 1 Thess 2:17–3:6.

18:2–3 Two of Paul's letters reflect his close association with Aquila and Priscilla. Not only does 1 Cor 16:8 note their presence with Paul in Ephesus, but v. 19 extends their greetings to the Corinthian congregation. Thus it seems certain that they were personally acquainted with the members of that church, and likely that they had met Paul during his founding visit to that city. Later, in Rom 16:3 it is Paul who sends greetings to them. So the couple was in Rome when Paul composed his letter to the Christian congregation in the capitol of the Roman Empire. A quite reasonable explanation of the couple's presence in Rome at this time is that after having been expelled in the year 41 CE they returned to Rome near the end of Claudius' reign (41–54 CE). All this renders it plausible that Paul met them in Corinth around 41 CE.

Paul's mention of the couple in 1 Cor 16:19, where "together with the church in their house" they send greetings to the Corinthians, permits the presumption that they were personally acquainted with the members of the Corinthian community. Since at the time of the writing of 1 Corinthians 16 they are with Paul in Ephesus (see v. 8), it is most probable that they made Paul's acquaintance during his founding visit in Corinth.

The phrase "together with the church in their house" affords us a glimpse of the couple's economic status. For whether the expression refers to a congregation that met in their home or to their household as a congregation,[148] it is clear that the couple is affluent. Therefore we can establish as probable not only the tradition that Paul met Priscilla and Aquila in Corinth, but also the information preserved in Acts 18 that Paul worked with them in Corinth. That Paul performed manual labor in Corinth is firmly attested by his own words.[149] The couple's affluence allowed them to employ others, among them Paul, in whom they would see both a Jewish and a Christian comrade. This also implies that they were already Christians when they came to Corinth.

In Rom 16:4, Paul gives the couple special praise for aiding him: they literally "risked their necks" for his life. We may therefore assume that this action was connected with the persecutions that Paul encountered in the vicinity of Ephesus.[150] This assistance and their mention in 1 Cor 16:19 presuppose their presence in Ephesus until shortly before Paul's third and final visit to Corinth. Since Paul wrote Romans during that visit, the couple's emigration to Rome must have occurred not long before the composition of that letter. Their return to their old residence would have had great importance for Paul's missionary plans.

18:5 The arrival of Silas and Timothy from Thessalonica in Corinth occurred during Paul's founding visit to Corinth. Paul confirms this:

> Timothy comes to Paul in Corinth from Thessalonica. (1 Thess 3:6)
> Brothers from Macedonia (including Timothy?) helped Paul during his stay at Corinth. (2 Cor 11:9; cf. also Phil 4:17)
> Paul, Silvanus, and Timothy sent greetings in the first verse of 1 Thessalonians, which was composed in Corinth.

That Timothy and Paul did not arrive in Corinth at the same time is evident from 1 Thess 3:6, which indicates that Paul was already present in Corinth when Timothy arrived there from Thessalonica. Thus, not only is the order of events in the first part of Acts 18 shown to be correct (first Paul worked with Priscilla and Aquila, *then* Timothy arrived), but the chapter also correctly places Timothy and Silas in Corinth during the foundation visit.

Since Paul indicates in 2 Cor 11:8–9 that he received money from the Philippians during his initial mission to Corinth,[151] Timothy was very likely part of the delegation that brought him the funds. Paul's statement that he had sent Timothy to Thessalonica from Athens[152] does not contradict this view, for Timothy could well have planned to make an excursion to Philippi during his visit to Thessalonica.

The Lukan flavoring of the report in Acts 18:5—that after Timothy and Silas arrived from Macedonia, Paul "devoted himself entirely to proclaiming the word"—could well reflect a redacted form of a tradition on the arrival of Timothy that included a monetary gift from the Philippian congregation. The circumstances and purpose of the monetary gift from Philippi, however, take on new significance when we combine Paul's letters and Acts at this point: Timothy apparently played an active role in receiving and delivering this gift, the purpose of which was to relieve Paul of the necessity of supporting himself and thus allow him to concentrate fully on missionary work.

18:8 And since 1 Cor 1:14 also mentions Crispus, this third element of the tradition contained in vv. 5–8 (see above) also derives from the first visit to Corinth. In 1 Cor 1:14 Paul remarks that contrary to his custom of not baptizing, he baptized Crispus and Gaius (the latter is not mentioned in Acts), and the context of this statement indicates that this baptism must have occurred during the founding visit. While the tradition in Acts does not explicitly say that Paul baptized Crispus, it nevertheless reports that Crispus' conversion and baptism occurred during the founding visit. This point of agreement speaks strongly in favor of the antiquity and reliability of the tradition about Crispus found in Acts.

18:12–17 *Gallio:* Though the foregoing analysis omits the report of Paul's trial before Gallio, I assume that a reference to Gallio must have been part of a tradition concerning Paul's activity in Corinth. Such an assumption follows from the reconstruction of a chronology based solely on Paul's authentic letters. Indeed, such a chronology includes a stay in Corinth during Gallio's tenure as a proconsul of Achaia from 51 to 52 CE.[153] Yet any such judicial hearing cannot have occurred during the foundation of the community, but only—if at all—on the occasion of a later visit of Paul. Since no tradition about a hearing or trial before Gallio can be recovered, one may doubt that anything of that sort ever took place, especially since Paul is not reported to have said a single word in his own defense.

Sosthenes: Since despite Acts 13:5 synagogues normally had but one "ruler" at a time,[154] the identification of Sosthenes as head of the synagogue must reflect a tradition differing in chronological setting from the one naming Crispus as the synagogue official who joined Paul and became a Christian. Unless Sosthenes was made ruler of the synagogue immediately after Crispus had joined Paul, the two probably represent different Pauline visits to Corinth. But since Luke was not an eyewitness in Corinth and had to rely on variant traditions, it is better not to assume that Sosthenes immediately replaced Crispus, but rather to see him in office at another time during Gallio's tenure as proconsul, especially since the two "rulers" appear in the same scene.

Finally, the Sosthenes named in 1 Cor 1:1 as the co-sender of the letter is unlikely to be the same person as the ruler of the synagogue in Corinth, for the latter remained a non-Christian Jew.

To come to the point, no other section of Acts contains so many historically accurate details, yet by attributing them to *a single* stay in Corinth and by incorrectly setting them after the Jerusalem conference, Luke has for nearly two millennia misled scholars. Fortunately, a critical reading of Paul's authentic letters provides us with the means to get the facts straight.

PRÉCIS: A NEW CHRONOLOGY OF PAUL

For reasons that will immediately become clear we must be ready to take into account chronological uncertainties ranging between two and four years. Besides, the possible date of Jesus' death ranges between 27 CE and 33 CE. Using the arithmetic average of 30 CE by no means guarantees its correctness. In short, I do not claim to offer a precise chronology; rather, the dates listed reflect an auxiliary construction that was drawn up to check the accuracy of Luke's information.

Let me now summarize the chronology outlined below and sketch its presuppositions: My chronology assumes the absolute priority in chronological matters of Paul's authentic letters over the book of Acts. It assumes three years as the interval between Jesus' death and Paul's conversion and two years between Paul's conversion and his first Jerusalem visit (twelve months in Damascus and one year for his mission among the Nabataeans in Arabia). Furthermore, it is based on the earlier conclusions that Paul's work in Greece

preceded the Jerusalem conference and that 1 Thessalonians belongs to the
early period of Paul's mission in Europe. The primary data supporting this
thesis and its far-reaching consequences are as follows:

1. In Phil 4:15 Paul explicitly states that the mission in Macedonia and
Achaia was in effect the real beginning of his preaching.

2. Acts 18 contains the tradition of two visits of Paul to Corinth, one of
which can be dated to 41 CE and the other to 51 CE.

3. At the Jerusalem conference around 48 CE Paul promises to organize
a collection for the Jerusalem congregation. Since we can plot the progress
of such a collection from passages in Romans, 1 Corinthians, 2 Corinthians,
and Galatians,[155] the conclusion may be drawn that these refer to one and the
same collection and that soon after the Jerusalem conference Paul did in fact
embark on a collection journey to his several churches in order to fulfill his
commitment. In that case he must have founded the Philippian, Thessalonian,
Corinthian, and Galatian congregations prior to the Jerusalem conference,
for it would have made no sense to agree to solicit funds from non-existent
communities. The only way to avoid such a conclusion would be to make the
seemingly incredible assumption that a previous collection had come to a halt
and was reinstituted after the founding of the above congregations.

Chronological Chart

30 CE	Crucifixion of Jesus
	Visions of the risen Jesus by Cephas
	(1 Cor 15:5)
	The Twelve (1 Cor 15:5)
	More than five hundred brothers (1
	Cor 15:6; Acts 2)
	James (1 Cor 15:7)
	All the apostles (1 Cor 15:7)
32–33	Conversion of Paul in Damascus
	Six-month stay in Damascus
	A year of mission in Arabia
	Return to Damascus for six months
	(Gal 1:15–17)
34	Paul's first visit to Jerusalem (the
	"Cephas visit," Gal 1:18)
	Journey to Syria and Cilicia (Gal 1:21)
	Mission there and in South Galatia
	together with Barnabas (Acts 13–14)
	Conversion of Timothy (1 Cor 4:17;
	Acts 16:1–3)

36–41	Independent mission in Europe: Philippi (1 Thess 2:2; Acts 16:12–40) Thessalonica (Phil 4:16; Acts 17:1–9) Failure in Athens (Acts 17:16–34; 1 Thess 3:1) Corinth (2 Cor 1:19: foundational preaching by Paul, Silvanus and Timothy)
39–40	*Emperor Caligula plans to have his statue erected in the Jerusalem temple.*
41	*The decree of Emperor Claudius regarding the Jews*
41	In Corinth Paul meets Aquila and Priscilla and works with them. (Acts 18:2) Paul stays in Corinth for eighteen months (Acts 18:11), during which time he composes 1 Thessalonians.
43	*Persecution of the church in Jerusalem by Herod Agrippa I.* Death of James, son of Zebedee (Acts 12:2) Peter escapes from prison and leaves Jerusalem. (Acts 12:17)
Circa 44	Paul founds Galatian congregations in the northern part of the Roman province (Gal 3:1; Acts 16:2)[156] when he was detained there by an illness. (Gal 4:13)
48	Paul's second visit to Jerusalem and conference with "the pillars" (Gal 2:1–11/Acts 15:6–29), followed by the journey to the already extant Pauline congregations for the organization of the collection
48	Incident at Antioch (Gal 2:11–14; Acts 15:1–2) shortly after or before the Jerusalem conference
49	Paul's second visit to Galatia (Gal 4:13) and organization of the collection there (1 Cor 16:1)

49–53	Paul in Ephesus (1 Cor 15:32; 16:8; Acts 19)
49	Timothy sent to Macedonia and Corinth (1 Cor 4:17) with the earliest but no longer extant letter to the Corinthians (1 Cor 6:9), containing instructions about the collection—unless those instructions were sent by messenger.
50–51	Timothy in Macedonia
51–52	*Gallio's term as proconsul of Achaia*
51 Spring	Letter to Paul from the Corinthians with questions regarding the collection—unless those questions were delivered orally (1 Cor 16:1)
51 around Easter	Composition of 1 Corinthians
51 between Easter and summer	Timothy in Corinth
51 Summer	After Timothy's bad news about Corinth upon returning to Paul in Ephesus, Paul makes a short intervening visit to Corinth. (cf. 2 Cor 2:1; 12:21; 13:2) "Paul before Gallio" (Acts 18:12–17) Precipitate return to Ephesus "Letter of tears" (2 Cor 2:3–9; 7:8–12) Sending of Titus to Corinth
51–52 Winter	Paul in danger of his life (imprisonment in Ephesus, 2 Cor 1:8) Composition of Philemon and Philippians (or else composition of both letters in Rome between 58 and 60 CE)
52 Spring	Paul's journey with Timothy from Ephesus to Troas (2 Cor 2:12) Further journey to Macedonia
52 Summer	Arrival of Titus in Macedonia from Corinth (2 Cor 7:6–7) Bad news from Galatia Composition of 2 Corinthians 1–9 and 10–13, and Galatians Sending of Titus with parts of 2

	Corinthians to Corinth in order to complete the collection
52–53 Winter	Paul in Macedonia and completion of the collection there
53 Spring/Summer	Paul journeys with Macedonian escorts to Corinth; completion of the collection there (Rom 15:26)
53–54 Winter	Paul in Corinth; composition of Romans
53–55	*Felix procurator in Judea* ("two years": Acts 24:27 [?])
54 Spring	Paul's third journey to Jerusalem to deliver the collection ("collection visit," Rom 15:25; Acts 21:17–19)
55–62	*Festus' term as procurator in Judea*
55–57	Imprisonment of Paul in Caesarea (Acts 24:27 [?])
57	Journey as a prisoner to Rome (Acts 27)

NOTES

1. On this topic see Lüdemann, *Paul—Apostle to the Gentiles*; Lüdemann, *Paul: The Founder*, 22–64; Lüdemann, *The Acts of the Apostles*. In this appendix I have freely borrowed from my works just mentioned. Riesner, *Paul's Early Period*, 3–32, presents a convenient history of the study of Pauline Chronology (until 1998) with helpful information about "Knox and His Students" (14–18).

2. See Lüdemann, *Paul—Apostle to the Gentiles*, 289–94, which answers responses to my work (until 1994). Jewett, *A Chronology of Paul's Life*, and Suhl, *Paulus*, willy-nilly treat Acts and Paul's letters as sources of the same rank and therefore have little new to contribute. Important are Hurd, *The Earlier Letters*, 9–45, and Hurd, *The Origin of I Corinthians*. So are also Hyldahl, *Die paulinische Chronologie*, Murphy-O'Connor, *St. Paul's Corinth*, and Tatum, *New Chapters*.

3. Knox' first article, "'Fourteen Years Later,'" was written in Nashville, where Knox from 1929 to 1936 served as Chaplain at Fisk University. (On his work at Fisk see Knox, *Never Far from Home*, 62–81.) Knox composed the second article, "The Pauline Chronology," in Chicago, to which he had returned in the summer of 1936. See further Knox, "Reflections." Among other subjects, Knox here deals with the relationship of his two essays to the book *Paul—Man of Conflict* by his teacher Riddle, to whom many scholars erroneously attributed the new chronology. See Lüdemann, *Paul—Apostle to the Gentiles*, 29 n. 3.

4. Rainer Riesner has become the main spokesperson of the traditional view that Paul's missionary work in Greece started around 50 ce. His massive and learned book,

Paul's Early Period, is helpful as a sort of lexicon. Alas, it is uncritical (see occasional quotes throughout this book).

5. Cf. Furnish, *1 Thessalonians*, 27: Paul's arrival in Thessalonica "is plausibly dated to the spring or summer of 49, and his departure to the autumn or early winter of the same year." After that Furnish refers approvingly to Malherbe, *The Letters to the Thessalonians*, 71–74 whose comments on the date of 1 Thessalonians do not belong to the strongest parts of his book. See further Ehrman, *The New Testament*, 324: 1 Thessalonians "is usually dated to about the year 49 c.e."

6. See Lüdemann, *Paul—Apostle to the Gentiles*, 163–64.

7. Cf. 1 Cor 16:8; Acts 18:18–19:1.

8. Cf. 2 Cor 2:12; 7:6–7; Acts 20:1.

9. Cf. Rom 15:26–27; Acts 21:15–17.

10. Gal 2:10.

11. This thesis combines Gal 1:21 and Acts 13–14.

12. Cf. Acts 15:39; Gal 2:11.

13. Cf. Phlm 9: Paul calls himself an "elderly man" (*presbytês*), and thus according to Hippocrates' definition would have been 50–56 years old. See Bauer, *A Greek-English Lexicon*, 707b.

14. "The fourteen-year 'silent' period is an obvious major fault in the traditional chronologies" (Knox, "Chapters in a Life of Paul," 363).

15. Rom 11:13.

16. Knox, "Rom 15:14–33 and Paul's Apostolic Mission," 7.

17. Acts 11:25; 12:25.

18. More on this below; see the interpretive note on Acts 18:2.

19. Cf. Riesner, *Paul's Early Period*, 327–33 ("Excursus II: Acts and World History").

20. Josephus, *Antiquities* 17.355.

21. Josephus, *Antiquities* 18.1ff.

22. Josephus, *Antiquities* 20,97ff., has Theudas enter public life at the time of the procurator Fadus (ca. 44 ce). According to Acts 5:36–37 this occurred before Gamaliel's speech, even before the census (6 bce), and Judas the Galilean supposedly appeared during the days of the census *after* Theudas.

23. Cf. Riesner, *Paul's Early Period*, 127–34.

24. Cf. "in those days" (Luke 2:1); "in these days" (Acts 6:1; 11:27); "about that time" (Acts 12:1; 19:23); "after many days" (Acts 9:23); "after some days" (Acts 15:36).

25. Cf. Hurd, *The Origin of I Corinthians*, 22.

26. Acts 11:26–15:41.

27. Acts 16–28.

28. Cf. Hurd, *The Origin of I Corinthians*, 23.

29. Wendland, *Die hellenistisch-römische Kultur*, 325 n. 5.

30. In Luke 3:14 John the Baptist tells soldiers, "Rob no one by violence or by false accusation, and be content with your wages," thus indicating that they should be loyal to the Roman state.

31. Cf. Lüdemann, "Acts of Impropriety," 69–71.

32. Baur, *Paulus*, vol. 1, 4–5. The first German edition was published 1845.

33. Knox, *Chapters in a Life of Paul*, 33 (2d ed., 19). Similarly, Riddle, *Paul—Man*

of Conflict, 9: A "correct picture of Paul is to be derived only from primary sources."

34. Talbert, *Reading Luke-Acts*, 205–6, refers to Lyons, *Pauline Autobiography*, and to J. T. Sanders, "Paul's 'Autobiographical' Statements," to suggest that Paul's remarks in Galatians 1–2 should be considered suspect.

35. I realize that in ancient autobiographical literature persons made assurances of truthfulness while at the same time compromising the truth; my argument with respect to Paul, however, is based on the specific nature and details of his situation.

36. On the Jerusalem origin of the opponents in Galatia, see Lüdemann, *Opposition to Paul*, 97–103.

37. E. P. Sanders, "Contribution" in Corley, *Colloquy on New Testament Studies*, 329, sketches well the methodological importance of Paul's statements in connection with his self-defense: "Although Paul's evidence on the number of trips to Jerusalem and other such things on which chronology is based does arise in a polemical context, it does not mean that the matters of fact which one may infer are wrong. On the contrary, as in the court case, one may take a testimony that is written for one purpose and employ it for another. That is, one may derive information from it and that information may be in fact more securely based than the information that would occur in a book such as Acts."

38. Acts 9:26–30; 11:30; 15:4; 18:22; 21:15–17.

39. Gal 6:12.

40. Gal 4:10.

41. Cf. Gal 1:23.

42. Donfried, *Paul, Thessalonica, and Early Christianity*, 103.

43. Luke's story that Paul went from Jerusalem bearing commissions from the High Priest to arrest Christians there (Acts 9:1–2) is as patently false as his earlier report that Paul was among those who murdered Stephen (Acts 7:57–8:1).

44. Hengel and Schwemer, *Paul between Damascus and Antioch*, 110.

45. Jewett, *A Chronology of Paul's Life*, 30–33.

46. See the full analysis by Welborn, "Paul's Flight from Damascus," 40–53.

47. Suhl, *Paulus*, 315. Cf. Donfried, *Paul, Thessalonica, and Early Christianity*, 113.

48. Cf. Acts 9:30.

49. Sanders, *Paul*, 9.

50. Knox, *Chapters in a Life of Paul*, 58 (2d ed., 41). The claim that Paul would have mentioned an early Macedonian mission there if he had gone to Greece prior to the Jerusalem conference is an argument from silence and hardly convincing. Cf. Lüdemann, *Paul—Apostle to the Gentiles*, 59, 291.

51. Meaning that they made no demands that Paul alter his message or the religious praxis required of his converts.

52. Gal 2:3.

53. The "incident at Antioch" which Paul narrates in Gal 2:11–13 proves that at one time Jewish and Gentile Christians ate together without observing the dietary law. This incident occurred before or after the Jerusalem conference. In my book *Paul—Apostle of the Gentiles*, 75–77, I have suggested that this event belongs to the time before the Jerusalem conference. I hope that scholars will not consider the proposed chronology to have been refuted if the occurrence at Antioch should be shown to belong actually to the period after the conference. The chronological place of Gal 2:11–13 is of little importance for the date of Paul's mission in Greece.

54. Gal 2:3; cf. 2:14 and 6:12.

55. Some would not even rule out the possibility that Paul eventually gave in to their demand, without being *forced* to do so. See Lüdemann, *Paul—Apostle to the Gentiles*, 72.

56. Cf. Bornkamm, *Paul*, 37–42, 97–101.

57. Neh 10:33.

58. See Isa 2:2-4; 60:3, 11–22; Mic 4:1–5; Jer 3:17; 16:19.

59. Berger, "Almosen," 200.

60. *mnêmoneuô*.

61. Minear, "The Jerusalem Fund," 391.

62. Bultmann, "Ethische und mystische Religion," 730.

63. Georgi, *Remembering the Poor*, 49.

64. Georgi, *Remembering the Poor*, 187 n. 1.

65. Georgi, *Remembering the Poor*, 45.

66. Georgi, *Remembering the Poor*, 43.

67. Gal 2:11–13.

68. Georgi, *Remembering the Poor*, 46.

69. Cf. Georgi, *Remembering the Poor*, 49–59.

70. Galatians 3/Romans 4; cf. also Gal 4:1–6 with Rom 8:2–16.

71. *pseudadelphoi*.

72. *katadoleô*.

73. *katesthiô*.

74. *aggelos*.

75. Borse, *Der Standort*, 86.

76. *eudokeô*.

77. "What do I gain if, humanly speaking, I fought with beasts in Ephesus?" (1 Cor 15:32)

78. "I will stay in Ephesus until Pentecost." (1 Cor 16:8)

79. 1 Cor 16:8.

80. 2 Cor 7–8.

81. 1 Cor 4:18.

82. 1 Cor 5:9.

83. 1 Cor 3:6.

84. 1 Cor 16:12.

85. 1 Cor 12, 14.

86. *hikanoi*.

87. 1 Cor 11:30.

88. 1 Cor 4:19.

89. 1 Cor 15:32a.

90. Hurd, *The Origin of I Corinthians*, 233.

91. Literally, "in the beginning of the gospel." NRSV reads: "In the early days of the gospel." The above translation "in the early days of my mission" is offered by *The New English Bible*, 2d ed.

92. *Pace* Jewett, *A Chronology of Paul's Life*, 82: Phil 4:15 "is surely a reference to the start of the Macedonian ministry."

93. *nomen actionis* (Latin).

94. See Bauer, *A Greek-English Lexicon*, 318.

95. *archê.*

96. Conzelmann, *Theologie,* 207–14.

97. See further Suggs, "Concerning the Date of Paul's Macedonian Ministry" and the comprehensive survey by Reumann, *Philippians,* 660–62.

98. Rom 15:20.

99. 1 Cor 3:10.

100. 1 Cor 3:6.

101. Phil 4:16.

102. 1 Thess 2:9.

103. 1 Cor 4:12a.

104. See above, 50–59.

105. See the comprehensive report in Funk and Hoover, *The Five Gospels.*

106. Klein, "Apokalyptische Naherwartung," 251.

107. Corley, *Colloquy on New Testament Studies,* 333.

108. Even the first apocalyptic teacher "is convinced that he will experience the end of times; this conviction is maintained throughout the ages" (Volz, *Eschatologie,* 136).

109. Knox, "The Pauline Chronology," 261–62.

110. Knox, "The Pauline Chronology," 262.

111. Rom 15:20.

112. Cf. v. 17.

113. Cf. Luke 2:1; Acts 8:1; 11:28; 21:30.

114. Cf. Luke 1:5; 2:1–2; 3:1.

115. Acts 11:28.

116. Cf. Acts 9:22; 17:3; 18:28.

117. Cf. Acts 13:51.

118. Josh 2:19; Judg 9:24; 2 Sam 1:16; 1 Kgs 2:32; Ezek 33:4.

119. Acts 13:46.

120. Cf. Acts 16:9.

121. See Luke 5:1; Acts 11:1; 13:5, 46; 16:32.

122. Acts 21:21, 24, 28; cf. 22:3; 24:14; 25:8; 28:17.

123. Cf. Acts 23:29; 25:18.

124. Cf. Hurd, *The Origin of I Corinthians,* 29–31.

125. *prosphatôs* occurs only here in the whole New Testament.

126. As the eighteen months "constitute for Acts an unusually long time for a Pauline stay" (Lampe, *From Paul to Valentinus,* 14), they likely stem from tradition.

127. Thus recently Dewey et al., *The Authentic Letters,* 200, 203.

128. Translation following J. C. Rolfe, LCL. "Chrestus" was a common slave name meaning "useful." It was often identified with "Christus" (Jesus).

129. Recently it has been claimed that "Chrestus" was the name of a Jewish disturber and not Jesus Christ. Thus Slingerland, *Claudian Policy Making,* 203–17 ("Chrestus and the Christus"). This view, however, is improbable, especially since *Chrestus* was used for *Christus* in popular language. Even if *Chrestus* was the name of a Jewish disturber in Rome, and Claudius' edict was intended to suppress an uprising that involved this Chrestus, Christians were nevertheless in danger of being expelled from Rome, for the Roman officials considered them Jews.

130. Translation by F. Stanley Jones.

131. See Lüdemann, *Paul—Apostle to the Gentiles*, 186 n. 64.

132. Ehrman, *The New Testament*, 374.

133. Cf. Haensch, "Das Statthalterarchiv."

134. Cf. Lüdemann, "Das Judenedikt."

135. Translation following E. Cary, LCL.

136. Cf. Murphy-O'Connor, *St. Paul's Corinth*, 155–58.

137. Translation following E. Cary, LCL. However, I have employed the same English verb for the anti-Jewish actions of the emperors and replaced "banished" by "drove out" because in the Greek texts of 57.18.5a and 60.6.6 the same verb, *exairein*, is used. Besides, we have the text of Dio's *Roman History* 57.18.5a only as a quotation by the Christian writer John of Antioch (seventh century ce).

138. See Mommsen, *Judaea*, 45.

139. Schürer, *The History of the Jewish People*, vol. 3, pt. 1, 77 n. 91.

140. Millar, *A Study of Dio Cassius*, 179.

141. Fitzmyer, *First Corinthians*, 39.

142. See Lüdemann, *Paul—Apostle to the Gentiles*, 163–64.

143. Lampe, *From Paul to Valentinus*, 15.

144. Lampe, *From Paul to Valentinus*, 15.

145. Lampe, *From Paul to Valentinus*, 15.

146. Botermann, *Das Judenedikt*, 56.

147. See Leon, *The Jews of Ancient Rome*, 25. Yet, according to Chineira, *Die Religionspolitik*, 195 n. 172, it "cannot be concluded from Tacitus' silence, as is often done, that Dio's report has priority over that of Suetonius." *Counter-argument:* For one thing, Chineira underestimates the weight of the silence of Tacitus on this point. For another, the question of priority between Dio's and Suetonius' account is a moot point, because they do not contradict one another here.

148. Rom 16:5 should certainly be understood in this sense.

149. 1 Cor 4:12; cf. 1 Thess 2:9.

150. See 1 Cor 15:32; 2 Cor 1:8–9.

151. Cf. also Phil 4:17.

152. 1 Thess 3:1–2.

153. See Lüdemann, *Paul—Apostle to the Gentiles*, 163–64.

154. See Barrett, *Acts*, 1:629.

155. Philippians, 1 Thessalonians and Philemon do not mention the collection.

156. Indeed, similarities of Galatians to 2 Corinthians 10–13 and Romans render the "north Galatia hypothesis" likelier than the "south Galatia hypothesis."

Appendix 2

1 Thessalonians 2:13–16

No other exegetical contribution of the last four decades has advocated the non-authenticity of 1 Thess 2:13–16 as forcefully as that of Birger A. Pearson.[1] Should Pearson's thesis be correct, it would have serious consequences for the interpretation of Paul's first extant writing and for my own view of this letter. Therefore, in addition to my earlier commentary on this section, I feel compelled to present further counter-arguments.

1. Pearson finds "it . . . virtually impossible to ascribe to Paul the *ad hominem* fragment of Gentile anti-Judaism in v. 15. Paul seems to have been rather proud of his achievements in Judaism prior to his 'conversion' (Gal. 1:14; Phil. 3:5f.)" (85).

Counter-argument: After his "conversion" and especially after law-observing Jewish Christians such as the "false brethren" of Gal 2:4 had attempted to disrupt his hard work, Paul directed sharp invectives against Judaism and even referred to its teachings and practices as "dung" (Phil 3:9). Paul labeled other Jews who sought to undermine his labors "the disobedient in Judea"[2] against whose enmity he asks the Romans to join him in praying for his safety and the success of his plans. Since "*ad hominem*" attacks have been launched against him and his missionary efforts, it is hardly difficult to imagine that Paul might harbor a degree of animus against those who launched them and express his feelings accordingly.

2. Pearson points to the contradiction between 1 Thess 2:14–16 (esp. 1 Thess 2:16: "The wrath has come upon them until the end")[3] and Romans 9–11 (esp. Rom 11:26: "all Israel will be saved") (85–86).

Counter-argument: The contradiction may be due to a change of heart or spiritual evolution on Paul's part: to put it idiomatically, he could have "mellowed." Or it could represent a tactical shift prompted by the possibility of a large number of ethnic Jews in the community at Rome. "Clearly, it is wrong simply to *assume* that Paul was absolutely consistent in what he thought and how he expressed his thinking, or that his views on any given topic never changed or developed."[4]

3. Pearson considers it improbable that Paul "would cite the Judaean Christians as examples for his Gentile Christian congregations" (87).

Counter-argument: This view does not take into account that Paul's teaching is based on the idea of a church composed of both Jews and Gentiles. Further, Paul often reminds the Gentile Christians of the Jewish Christians.[5] Besides, the collection for the Saints in Jerusalem reflects his insistence on the close relationship between the Gentile and Jewish elements of the church. In Gal 2:7 Paul even speaks of "a gospel for the uncircumcised (Gentiles)" and "a gospel for the circumcised (Jews)." He presupposes that both parts of the church are "in Christ" and that this status derives from baptism into Christ.[6]

4. The authenticity of 1 Thess 2:13–16 depends on the historicity of significant persecutions of Palestinian Christians during the first Christian decade in Palestine, yet it is questionable whether such persecutions occurred (86–87).

Counter-arguments: For one thing, historical accounts attest to the anti-Christian persecution by Herod Antipas I that led to the killing of the apostle James.[7] For another, Paul's founding proclamation warned of impending persecution,[8] a prognosis that proved accurate. In such a context, the essentially theological statement we find in 1 Thess 2:15 hardly demands the level or degree of persecution that Pearson's objection presupposes. Last but not least, Paul himself once persecuted the Jewish Christian church[9] and got persecuted after his "conversion."[10]

5. The term "imitator" in 1 Thess 2:14 ("you became imitators of the churches of God in Christ Jesus which are in Judea") does not match the usual meaning of "imitator" in Paul's letters (87–88).

Counter-arguments: To be sure, nowhere else in the extant Pauline letters do we find a reference to one church imitating another, but rather the injunction that Christians should imitate Paul.[11] Indeed, an earlier passage of this letter, 1 Thess 1:6, speaks about imitating Paul, and this imitation clearly corresponds to that among the churches—especially since in both passages Paul emphasizes a common outcome to suffering. In 1 Thess 1:6 the imitation consists in the reception of the word in the context of "great affliction," while in 2:14 the Thessalonians are said to imitate the churches in Judea by their common suffering of what Paul in both 1:6 and 3:3a calls "persecutions."[12] In fact, this application of the concept of imitation suggests a common experience of churches and considerably enriches our understanding of Paul's theme. It is yet another reason to assume the integrity of 1 Thess 2:13–16.

6. According to Pearson, form-critical analyses suggest that 1 Thess 2:13–16 is an interpolation, because 2:17–3:13 is by this means identifiable as an apostolic *parousia*[13] with 1 Thess 2:11–12 as its introduction (89–90).

Counter-arguments: 1 Thess 2:11–12 does not introduce the section 2:17–3:13, but rather concludes the section 2:1–10, for in 2:11–12 Paul continues the account of his work *in Thessalonica* (v. 12a) and as a conclusion describes the goal of his efforts: that the Thessalonians might "walk in ways worthy of

God, who calls you into his own kingdom and glory" (v. 12b). It should also be noted that while verses 1–12 deal primarily with Paul's behavior toward the members of the community, vv. 13–16 shift to a concern the community's reception of the gospel message.

In summary, it appears evident beyond serious doubt that 1 Thess 2:13–16 derives from the historical Paul. However unpalatable the thought may be to some, and counter-intuitive as it may seem, he expressed and even promoted enmity against non-Christian Jews in his earliest letter, and did so in a way that eclipsed any other verbal attack on non-Christian Jews by Christians during the first three centuries of the Common Era.

NOTES

1. Pearson, "1 Thessalonians 2:13–16." See the assent by Boers, "The Form Critical Study," 150–52; Schmidt, "1 Thess 2.13–16: Linguistic Evidence." From among recent English speaking commentaries the one by Richard, *First and Second Thessalonians*, 119–27, agrees to Pearson's thesis. For a criticism see Scott, "Paul's Use of Deuteronomic Tradition," 651–56; Lyons, *Pauline Autobiography*, 202–7; Luckensmeyer, *The Eschatology of First Thessalonians*, 161–67; Donfried, *Paul, Thessalonica, and Early Christianity*, 198 n. 22. Cf. also Jewett, *The Thessalonian Correspondence*, 36–42; Furnish, *1 Thessalonians*, 64–67.

2. Rom 15:31.

3. Pearson writes: "God's wrath has come upon the Jewish people with utter finality" (85–86).

4. Furnish, *1 Thessalonians*, 67.

5. Cf. Rom 15:27; Gal 1:22–23.

6. Gal 3:26; Rom 16:7.

7. Acts 12:1–2. On the historical value of this passage see Lüdemann, *The Acts of the Apostles*, 154–63.

8. Cf. 1 Thess 3:4.

9. 1 Cor 15:8; Gal 1:13, 23; Phil 3:6.

10. 2 Cor 11:24; cf. Sanders, *Paul, the Law, and the Jewish People*, 191.

11. 1 Cor 4:16; 11:1; Phil 3:17.

12. Cf. Schade, *Apokalyptische Christologie*, 124–26, 263–64.

13. Cf. Funk, "The Apostolic *Parousia*," 250.

Appendix 3

Romans 9–11

Earlier we identified hatred of "non-believing" Jews as characteristic of the early Paul, and pointed out that he may later have abandoned this attitude (see above, 4–6). While this animosity is patent in his earliest extant letter, its relationship to his later assurance of solidarity requires further reflection. The section Romans 9–11, in which Paul examines his bond with these unconverted compatriots, offers a suitable text for examining the situation. Paul's reflections had already begun in Rom 3:1 ("What advantage has the Jew?") but were dropped in Rom 3:8 only to be picked up again in Rom 9:1.

With these questions in mind I offer a translation with commentary.[1] As elsewhere, I have employed cross references to foster a discerning reading of the text and facilitate exegesis. In addition, I have used indentation to indicate quotations and traditional material.

ROMANS 9:1–5
Introduction: The Unbelief of Israel

[1] I am speaking the truth in Christ, I am not lying; my conscience bears me witness in the Holy Spirit, [2] that there is great pain and unceasing anguish in my heart. [3] For I could pray that I myself were separated by a curse from Christ for the sake of my brothers, my fellow citizens by ethnic descent [4] who are Israelites:

> to whom belong the adoption as God's children and the glory and the covenants,
> and the giving of the law and the worship and the promises;
> [5] to whom belong the Fathers,
> and from whom, by ethnic descent, is the Christ.

> God who is over all be blessed forever. Amen.

9:1 *Christ* 1:3, 5; 10:4, 6–7, 17.
9:3 *Brothers* 10:1; 11:25a. *Ethnic descent* 9:5, 8.
9:4 *Israel, Israelites* 9:6, 27, 31; 10:19, 21; 11:1, 7, 25b, 26a. *God* 9:5–6, 8, 11, 14, 16, 20, 22, 26; 10:1–3, 9; 11:1–2, 8, 21–23, 29–30, 32–33. *Children* 9:7–8, 10. *Glory* 9:23; 11:36. *Law* 9:31; 10:4–5. *Promise* 9:8–9.
9:5 *Fathers* 11:28. *All* 11:26a, 32, 36. *Amen* 11:36.

The beginning of Romans 9 is exceedingly abrupt. After asserting in Rom 8:39b that nothing will be able "to separate us from the love of God in Christ Jesus our Lord," Paul turns to his unbelieving fellow Jews, on whose account he says he feels such great pain that he would renounce his own faith if he thought that doing so would save them.[2] The reason for this less than explicitly detailed wish is that despite the gifts (listed in v. 4) by which God has bound himself to them, the overwhelming majority of Jews have not accepted the gospel.[3]

But what is the status of those gifts? Will God keep his word? In the following Paul engages in quite complicated interpretations of Scripture that are often difficult to follow. For the sake of simplification I have divided Paul's exegetical endeavors into three answers to the problem at hand.

ROMANS 9:6–29
The First Answer

[6]But it is not as though the word of God had failed.

For not all from Israel are Israel,

[7]and not all the children of Abraham are his offspring; but

Through Isaac shall your offspring be named.
[Gen 21:12 LXX]

[8]This means that it is not the children of ethnic descent who are the children of God, but the children of the promise are counted as offspring. [9]For this is what the promise said,

About this time I will come
and Sarah shall have a son.
[Gen 18:10, 14]

[10]And that is not all, for when Rebecca had conceived children by one [husband], our Father Isaac, [11]though they were not yet born and had done nothing either good or bad—so that God's purpose of election might remain, [12]not because of works but because of his call—she was told,

The elder will be slave to the younger.
[Gen 25:23 LXX]

[13]As it is written,

Jacob I loved, but Esau I hated.
[Mal 1:2–3 LXX]

[14]What shall we say then? Is there unrighteousness on God's part? Not at all! [15]For to Moses he says,

---

9:6 *Word* 10:8, 17; 10:18.
9:7 *Abraham* 11:1. *Offspring* 9:8; 9:29; 11:1. *Isaac* 9:10.
9:12 *Works* 11:6.
9:13 *Jacob* 11:26b.
9:15 *Moses* 10:5, 19. *Mercy, merciful* 9:16, 18, 23; 11:30–32.

> I will show mercy to whom I have mercy,
> and I will pity whom I pity.
> [Exod 33:19 LXX]

¹⁶So it does not depend on human will or effort, but on the merciful God. ¹⁷For in the scripture [God tells] Pharaoh,

> I have raised you up
> for the very purpose of showing my power in dealing with you,
> so that my name may be proclaimed throughout the earth.
> [Exod 9:16]

¹⁸So then he shows mercy to whomever he wishes, and he hardens the heart of whomever he wishes. ¹⁹You will ask me then, Why does he still find fault? For who can resist his will? ²⁰But who are you, a human being, to answer back to God?

> Will what is molded say to the molder,
> Why have you made me thus?
> [cf. Isa 29:16 LXX; 45:9]

²¹Has the potter no right over the clay, to make out of the same lump one vessel in honor and another in dishonor?

²²But what if God, wishing to show his wrath and to make known his power, has endured with much patience the vessels of wrath made for destruction ²³in order to make known the riches of his glory for the vessels of mercy, which he has prepared beforehand for glory?—²⁴Even us he has called, not from the Jews only but also from the Gentiles.

²⁵As indeed he says in Hosea,

> I will call that which is not my people "my people,"
> And that which is not loved "my beloved."
> [Hos 2:25]

> ²⁶And it will be that in the place where it was said to them,
> You are not my people,
> there they shall be called sons of the living God.
> [Hos 2:1 LXX]

²⁷But Isaiah cries out concerning Israel:

> When the number of the sons of Israel is like the sand of the sea,
> the remnant will be saved,
> [Isa 10:22; Hos 2:1 LXX]

> ²⁸for in executing his sentence upon the earth
> the Lord will act swiftly.
> [cf. Isa 10:22–23 LXX]

²⁹And as Isaiah foretold,

9:24 *Call* 9:25–26; 11:28. *Gentiles* 9:30; 11:1, 12–13, 25c.
9:27 *Isaiah* 9:29. *Remnant* 11:5.
9:28 *Lord* 9:29; 10:9, 13, 16; 11:3, 34.

> If the Lord of hosts
> had not left us offspring,
> we would have become like Sodom
> and been made like Gomorrah.
> [Isa 1:9 LXX]

The *first answer*, contained in Rom 9:6–29, expands the statement in v. 6: "But it is not as though the word of God had failed. For not all from Israel are Israel." In other words, ethnic descent does not guarantee salvation. Further, God's promise extends only to those who are chosen by God's free grace and his mercy according to his wish to bestow it (v. 15). "Israel as the object of election is to be distinguished from empirical Israel."[4]

In seeking to persuade his audience that God's promise of salvation extended not to the whole nation of Israel, but only a select group, Paul cites Scripture to the effect that only those of Abraham's offspring so chosen by God's gracious choice can properly be considered his children (vv. 7–8). To this he adds the analogic argument (vv. 20–23) that just as a potter can shape his raw material as he wishes, God is justified in dealing as he wants with his creatures: he may choose to save or condemn them.

At this point Paul is not indulging in theological speculation or offering a theory of predestination; his aim is to discard even the possibility of entertaining the notion of God's will being thwarted. Such a challenge is as inconceivable as having a lump of clay challenge a potter's decision on what to make with it. Matters of God's plan with the Jewish people simply cannot be subjected to intellectual inquiry. (One may sense a touch of irony in his use of that strategy in demonstrating this thesis.)

In v. 22 Paul refers to contemporary "unbelieving" Jews, and v. 23 to Christians. As "vessels of wrath" (v. 22), the former are already prepared for annihilation. In the manifestation of wrath, this predestination will be realized in final destruction.[5] According to this end-time perspective, God's primary preoccupation is not salvation, but rather damnation.

The sharpness of the avowals in vv. 22–23 should not be reduced by Paul's assurances in chapter 11. Moreover, still a positive aspect surfaces at this point: The Christians as vessels of mercy have been prepared beforehand for glory (v. 23); God has fulfilled his word of promise as it was originally intended by means of the church made up of Jews and Gentiles (v. 24).

ROMANS 9:30–10:21

The Second Answer

[30]What shall we say, then? Gentiles who do not pursue righteousness attained righteousness, that is, righteousness through faith; [31]but Israel who pursued

---

9:30 *Faith* 9:32; 10:4, 6, 8, 17; 11:20–22. *Righteousness* 9:31; 10:3–5, 10.

a law of righteousness did not reach that law. ³²Why? Because it was not through faith, but as if it were on the basis of works. They have stumbled over the stumbling stone, ³³as it is written,

> Look, I am laying in Zion a stone of stumbling,
> and a rock of offence;
> and whoever believes in him
> will not be put to shame.
> [Isa 28:16; 8:14]

^{10:1}Brothers, my heart's desire and prayer to God on their behalf is for their salvation. ²I bear them witness that they have a zeal for God, but it is without comprehension. ³For, being ignorant of the righteousness of God, and seeking to establish their own, they did not submit to God's righteousness. ⁴For Christ is the end of the law, that every one who has faith may be justified.

⁵For Moses writes about righteousness through the law,

> The person who practices (the commandments) shall live by it.
> [cf. Lev 18:5]

⁶But the righteousness through faith says,

> Do not say in your heart,
> [Deut 9:4]
> Who will ascend into heaven?
> [Deut 30:12]

that is, to bring Christ down,
⁷or

> Who will descend into the underworld?
> [cf. Deut 30:13; Ps 107:26]

that is, to bring Christ up from the dead.
⁸But what does it say?

> The word is near you,
> in your mouth and in your heart,
> [Deut 30:14]

that is, the word of faith we preach;
⁹because,

> if you confess with your mouth
> that Jesus is Lord,
> and believe in your heart
> that God raised him from the dead,
> you will be saved.

¹⁰For with the heart one believes for righteousness,
and with the mouth one confesses for salvation.
¹¹For the scripture says,

> No one who believes in him will be put to shame.
> [Isa 28:16]

10:9 *Believe* 10:10–11, 14, 16. *Salvation, save* 10:10, 13; 11:11, 14, 26a.

¹²For there is no distinction between Jew and Greek; the same Lord is Lord of all and is rich to all who call upon him. ¹³For,

> every one who calls upon the name of the Lord will be saved.
>
> [Joel 3:5]

¹⁴But how are they to call upon one in whom they have not believed? And how are they to believe in one of whom they have never heard? And how are they to hear without a preacher? ¹⁵And how are they to preach unless they are sent? As it is written,

> How timely are the feet of those who bring the Good!
>
> [Isa 52:7; Nah 2:1]

¹⁶But not all have obeyed the gospel; for Isaiah says, Lord, who has believed what he has heard from us? [Isa 53:1 LXX]

¹⁷So faith comes from hearing, and hearing comes through the word of Christ. ¹⁸But I ask, have they not heard? Indeed they have; for

> Their voice has gone out to all the earth,
> and their words to the ends of the world.
>
> [Ps 18:5 LXX]

¹⁹But I ask, did Israel not understand? Moses first says,

> I will make you jealous of those who are not a nation;
> with a foolish nation I will make you angry.
>
> [Deut 32:21 LXX]

²⁰But Isaiah boldly says,

> I was found by those who did not search for me;
> I became visible to those who did not ask for me.
>
> [Isa 65:1]

²¹But of Israel he says,

> All day long I have held out my hands
> to a people which is disobedient and obstinate.
>
> [Isa 65:2]

This *second answer* is that while Gentiles have attained righteousness (*dikaiosynê*) through faith (9:30), Israel has tripped and fallen (9:32b). It heard the gospel, the preaching of the good news of Christ (10:17–18), but sought to establish its righteousness through works (10:3).

For Paul, the Greek understanding of the word *dikaiosynê*—usually rendered "justice" or "righteousness" and indicating one of the four cardinal virtues[6]—is irrelevant. Paul, whose conceptual background is Judaism, holds in common with that faith tradition the notion that righteousness is the prereq-

---

10:19 *jealous* 11:11, 14.

uisite for salvation[7] and that possessing it depends on the end-time judgment of a heavenly arbiter. Paul adjusts this understanding, of course, insofar as he insists that for the faithful the judgment has already been made "in Christ" and that righteousness accrues on the basis of their faith alone and irrespective of virtuous deeds. Christ is the end of the law and God's righteousness, like his grace, is not a beneficent lenience, but rather the guarantee of salvation.[8]

In Rom 10:6–9 Paul employs a dialectical model of Jewish origin in which he frames and supplements the scriptural record with his own explications, and by implication assigns scriptural status to his glosses, further distorting each citation by an anachronistic explication. In v. 6, for example, he cites Deut 30:12, "Who will ascend to heaven?" and then adds, "that is, to bring Christ down." Next, in v. 7 he changes Deut 30:13 from "Who will go over to the sea?" to "Who will descend to the underworld?" and then appends an equally imaginative interpretation, "that is, to bring Christ up from the dead."

In this "second answer" Paul blames the rejection of Israel on the *guilt* of the Jewish people, who have themselves rejected the saving acts of God. They were offered salvation (10:18–19), but they failed to respond to the message that should have generated faith. The rejecters have been rejected.

ROMANS 11:1–36
The Third Answer

11:1I ask, then, has God cast off his people? By no means! I myself am an Israelite, an offspring of Abraham, a member of the tribe of Benjamin.

> 2God has not cast off his people
> [1 Sam 12:22; Ps 94:14]

whom he knew from before.

Or do you not know what the scripture says of Elijah, how he pleads with God against Israel?

> 3Lord, they have killed your prophets,
> they have demolished your altars,
> and I alone am left, and they seek my life.
> [1 Kings 19:10, 14]

4But what is the divine statement to him?

> I have kept for myself seven thousand
> who have not bowed the knee to Baal.
> [cf. 1 Kgs 19:18]

5So too at the present time there is a remnant, chosen by grace. 6But if it is by grace, it is no longer through works; otherwise grace would no longer be grace.

7What then? Israel failed to obtain what it sought. The chosen [NRSV: elect] obtained it, but the rest were hardened, 8as it is written,

> God gave them a spirit of stupor,

eyes that would not see
and ears that would not hear,
down to this very day.
[Deut 29:3; Isa 29:10]

[9]And David says,

Let their table become a snare and a trap,
a pitfall and a retribution for them;
[10]let their eyes be darkened so they cannot see,
and bend their backs forever.
[cf. Ps 68:23–24 LXX]

[11]I ask, then, have they stumbled in order that they should fall? Not at all! But through their stumbling, salvation has come to the Gentiles, so as to make them [the Jews] jealous.

[12]If their stumbling means wealth for the world, and
if their defeat means wealth for the Gentiles,
how much more will their full number mean!

[13]Now I am speaking to you Gentiles. Inasmuch then as I am an apostle to the Gentiles, I magnify my ministry [14]in order to make my people [lit: "my flesh"] jealous, and thus save some of them.

[15]For if their rejection means the reconciliation of the world,
what will their acceptance mean but life from the dead?

[16]If the dough offered as first fruits is holy,
so is the whole lump;
and if the root is holy,
so are the branches.

[17]But if some of the branches were broken off, and you, a wild olive shoot, were grafted in their place to share the richness of the olive tree, [18]do not boast over the branches. If you do boast, remember it is not you that support the root, but the root that supports you.

[19]You will say, Branches were broken off so that I might be grafted in.

[20]That is true. They were broken off because of their unbelief, but you stand fast only through faith.

So do not become proud, but stand in awe. [21]For if God did not spare the natural branches, neither will he spare you.

[22]Pay attention, then, to the kindness and the severity of God:
severity toward those who have fallen, but God's kindness to you,
if you remain in the sphere of his kindness; otherwise you too will be cut

11:16 *branches* 11:17–19, 21.
11:17 *Olive tree* 11:24, 27.

off. ²³And even those [the Jews] if they do not remain in their unbelief, will be grafted in, for God has the power to graft them in again.

²⁴For if you have been cut from what is by nature a wild olive tree, and grafted, contrary to nature, into a cultivated olive tree,

how much more will these who belong to him by nature be grafted back into their own olive tree!

^{25a}Lest you be wise in your own conceits, I do not want you to be ignorant concerning this mystery, brothers:

> ^{25b}a hardening has come in part upon Israel,
> ^{25c}until the full number of the Gentiles come in,
> ^{26a}and so all Israel will be saved; as it is written,
> > ^{26b}From Zion will come a Deliverer,
> > he will remove impiety from Jacob;
> > ²⁷and this will be my covenant with them
> > when I take away their sins.
> > [Isa 59:20–21; 27:9; Jer 31:33–34]

A ²⁸As regards the gospel they are enemies for your sake;
> B but as regards election they are beloved for the sake of the Fathers.
> > C ²⁹For the gifts and the call of God are irrevocable.

A' ³⁰Just as you were once disobedient to God but now have received mercy because of their disobedience,
> B' ³¹so they have now been disobedient in order that by the mercy shown to you they also may receive mercy.
> > C' ³²For God has imprisoned all in disobedience, that he may have mercy upon all.

³³O the depth of the wealth
and wisdom and knowledge of God!

How unfathomable are his judgments
and how untraceable his ways!
> > ³⁴For who knew the mind of the Lord,
> > or who became his adviser?
> > [Isa 40:3]
> > ³⁵Or who gave a gift to him
> > that he might be repaid?"
> > [Job 41:3]

³⁶For from him and through him and to him are all things.
To him be glory forever. Amen.

This *third answer* emphasizes that God's rejection of Israel is not definitive.

Paul is unwilling to accept the idea that God has cast off his people (11:1) even if the majority of them have become stubborn. "Paul suddenly asserts that God can*not* have rejected his people, ethnic Israel, after all (11:1–2). This is surprising given chapter 9. . . . Ethnic Israel is split into two—the chosen remnant and the hardened majority."[9]

The apostle therefore follows the Hebrew Prophets in their assurance of a remnant saved by grace (11:1–5); but his own historical context is such that he is obliged to demonstrate the realization of the promises by pointing to Jewish Christians.

11:11 Paul begins with the question of whether Israel's stumbling was intended to produce their fall. He rejects such a conclusion and proposes a positive consequence of Israel's "false step": inasmuch as the (majority of) Jews did not accept the gospel, salvation has come to the Gentiles. The whole section is addressed as a warning to the latter, the predominantly Gentile Christian readers and hearers of the letter in Rome.

11:12 If Israel's rejection of the gospel leads to the spiritual enrichment of the world and its defeat results in converts from among the Gentiles, the eventual addition of all Israel is of even greater value. The "full number" (of Jews) will include the present remnant of the Jewish Christians together with the majority of non-believing Jews. But how can the redemption of the full number be possible after the fall of the majority? The statement in vv. 25–26 will resolve this problem.

11:13–14 Thus Paul's office as apostle to the Gentiles consists in making those sharing his ethnic descent jealous[10] in order to save some of them.

11:15 Their recovery will be none other than God's deliverance of Israel at the end of times when the resurrection of the dead takes place.

11:16 Paul uses imagery to explain to the Gentile Christians their relationship to the Jews: "If the dough offered as first fruits is holy, so is the whole lump; and if the root is holy, so are the branches."

11:17–24 The image of the olive tree now shows what Paul sees as the paradoxical nature of God's work of salvation: through their unbelief the Jews are "cut off" from the olive tree, and God has replaced them by "grafting in" the Gentiles, thus making them children of Israel. But the Gentiles must not be arrogant towards Israel, since God can with equal ease replace the "unnatural" wild shoots and accept Israel again (vv. 23–24).

11:25–27 The idea of the reacceptance of unbelieving Israel, of its regrafting onto its native tree, permeates the whole section from v. 11 on. In v. 25a we find Paul once again creating a "mystery" (Recall that "I do not want to you to be ignorant" always introduces new information[11]) in order to buttress a dubious—but in his eyes essential—doctrine. His aim is to demonstrate the truth of the olive-tree metaphor, which represents his desperate hope that large numbers of both Jews and Gentiles can be persuaded to accept his new religion. Not only is there a chance for "non-believing" Jews to join the parade, but Gentile Roman Christians are again warned that they must not be smug and complacent. Note also that vv. 25b, 25c, and 26a establish a threefold pattern that will be repeated in vv. 28–32 (on which see below).

The mystery makes two statements: First, the hardening of Israel in part will last until "the full number of Gentiles" determined by God has come in. Second, all Israel, i.e. the Jews as people, will so be saved. In 11:26b–27 Paul supports his conclusion with prophecies from Isa 59:20 and Jer 31:33–34.[12] Note that the quotation consigns the salvation of "all Israel" to the Deliverer; "that is, it puts it outside the bounds of the apostolic missions altogether."[13] Thereby "faith in Christ" is no longer required—not even in the future at the arrival of the Deliverer—for nothing in the quotation (vv. 26–27) is connected with Christ. The Deliverer most likely refers to God,[14] and Christ has no part in the end-time scenario of Israel's salvation.

After the previous verses the statements of vv. 25–26 are new, even though in vv. 11–12, 15, 23–24 Paul had already—albeit as a remote historical possibility—hinted at the content of the "mystery" that all Israel, that is, the Jews as a people, will finally be saved. The other motif not previously introduced is the statement that the hardening of Israel will last until God has brought on board as many Gentiles as he desires.

Thus Paul is giving ethnic Israel an advantage.[15] According to the proof text in vv. 26–27, iniquity will be removed from Jacob—"that is, from the people of Israel as defined by physical descent."[16] And while Paul earlier rejected physical descent as a guarantee of salvation (Rom 9:6b: "Not all from Israel are Israel"), the failure of the mission among the Jews now seems to incline him to fully adopt it.[17]

Let me hasten to add that by using the phrase "all Israel will be saved" Paul employs a Jewish "creed." In Mishnah Sanhedrin 10:1 we read: "All Israel—there is for *them* a share in the world to come."[18] Only three groups are excluded: "He that says that there is no resurrection of the Dead prescribed in the Law, [he that says] that the Law is not from Heaven, and an Epicurean."[19]

By introducing this deeply Jewish view that "all Israel will be saved"[20] Paul puts the "non-believing" Jews on the same level as the "believing Jews" and the "believing Gentiles." In a moment of deep emotional turmoil he has rediscovered his mother-religion, ethnic Israel. And yet the special importance here assigned to the Jews appears artificial. "By this particular view his whole doctrine of faith is embarrassed, thrown into confusion, and rendered seriously inconsistent. . . . This discordant addition (for so it may be described) which the Apostle makes to his doctrine of Salvation runs across the very principle of his faith and even counteracts its convincing force."[21]

11:28–32 As suggested above on vv. 25–27, this section is a rhetorical product that expands on vv. 25b–26; and following the "mystery" therein announced, he certifies it with a scriptural citation and concludes the performance "with two balanced sentences, [marked A, B and A′, B′ in the text] each constructed on the same pattern. Each contains a pair of antithetical clauses explained by a 'for' (*gar*) clause,"[22] marked C, C'. Compare my translation above. The final message is that God will have mercy on all. "'All Israel' is to be understood along with 'all people' in verse 32 and 'everything' in verse 36. Israel is not singled out for salvation by a separate route, and distinguished from Gentiles, only some of whom are saved. Israel is simply a part of God's final victory, which will embrace the entire creation."[23]

This peroration is clearly a rhetorical flourish[24] aimed at consolidating Paul's résumé as a divinely appointed and inspired apostle; ironically, it also makes him look like a Stoic philosopher. Compare the statement of Marcus Aurelius, *Meditations* 4.23: "All things come *from* you [creator], all things exist *in* you, all things are destined *for* you."[25] A corollary irony, then, is that Paul seems to have placed a greater reliance on literary skill than on logical discourse. He has left the burning problem of Jews and Christians behind and lifts up his eyes. No wonder that he concludes Romans 9–11 with a doxology (vv. 33–36). The pain caused by the Jews' non-acceptance of the gospel is forgotten, and Paul the theologian has once again produced a winning argument by deceiving himself with his own salesmanship.

NOTES

1. I have benefited from Georg Strecker's exegeses of Romans 9–11 (see Strecker, *Theology of the New Testament*, 203–9) and from conversations with him during my student-days in Göttingen.

2. Cf. Moses' wish to make atonement for the sins of his people (Exodus 32:32).

3. Cf. Rom 10:16: "Not all have obeyed the gospel."

4. Conzelmann, *An Outline*, 250.

5. Cf. 1 Thess 2:16b.

6. Justice (*dikaiosynê*), prudence (*phronêsis*), fortitude (*andreia*), temperance (*sôphrosynê*).

7. Rom 1:17; 4:13; 5:17, 21; 8:10; Gal 3:6.

8. Cf. Conzelmann, *An Outline*, 217–18.

9. Räisänen, "A Controversial Jew," 32.

10. Cf. Rom 10:19; 11:1.

11. See Rom 1:13; cf. above, 72, n. 178.

12. It is worth noting that Jer 31:33–34 is the prophecy of the New Covenant, which elsewhere in the New Testament is always applied to the Church as the New Israel, and not, as here, to the salvation of the Jews. See Heb 8:8–12; Matt 26:28; Mark 14:24; Heb 10:16; John 6:45.

13. Sanders, *Paul, the Law, and the Jewish People*, 195.

14. The "Old Testament regards the earthly Zion as God's dwelling place (see, e.g., Pss 9:11; 50:2; Joel 3:17)" (Keck, *Romans*, 282).

15. Cf. Sanders, *Paul*, 125.

16. Sanders, *Paul*, 125.

17. Cf. Sanders, *Paul*, 125. However, according to Sanders (*Paul*, 125) from whose work on Paul and about Judaism I have immensely profited, the statement about "all

Israel" in Rom 11:26 does not contradict the explanation in Rom 11:23 about those Jews who do not remain in their unbelief and therefore are grafted in again into the olive tree.

18. Literal translation by Sanders, *Paul and Palestinian Judaism*, 182.

19. Sanders, *Paul and Palestinian Judaism*, 147. The later, clearly secondary exclusions that follow (10:2–4) need not concern us here.

20. Cf. already Isa 45:25; Testament of Benjamin 10:11.

21. Harnack, *The Date of Acts*, 48. Harnack further remarks: "To Gentile Christians of the next generations (and certainly also to contemporaries) the argument of Rom. xi must have been very unpleasing. They could only pass over it in silence, and this they did" (Harnack, *The Date of Acts*, 48–49 n. 2).

22. Barrett, *The Epistle to the Romans*, 207.

23. Sanders, *Paul*, 125–26.

24. Cf. the repeated use of "all" (*pas/panta*) in the final section of 1 Thessalonians (5:14, 15, 16, 18, 22) where it clearly serves a rhetorical purpose.

25. Adapted from Keck, *Romans*, 288.

Works Consulted

Ascough, Richard S. *Paul's Macedonian Associations: The Social Context of Philippians and 1 Thessalonians*. Tübingen: Mohr Siebeck, 2003.

Baldry, H. C. *The Unity of Mankind in Greek Thought*. Cambridge: University Press, 1965.

Bammel, Ernst. *Judaica et Paulina*. Tübingen: Mohr Siebeck, 1997.

Barclay, John M. G. *Pauline Churches and Diaspora Jews*. Tübingen: Mohr Siebeck, 2001.

Barrett, C. K. *A Critical and Exegetical Commentary on the Acts of the Apostles*. London: T & T Clark, 2004 [1st ed. 1994].

———. *The Epistle to the Romans*. London: Adam & Charles Black, ²1991.

Bauer, Walter. *A Greek-English Lexicon of the New Testament and Other Early Christian Literature*. 4th rev. and augmented ed., 1952. Cambridge: Cambridge University Press, 1957.

Baur, Ferdinand Christian. *Paulus, der Apostel Jesu Christi*. 2 vols. Herausgegeben von Eduard Zeller. Leipzig: Fues, 1866/1867.

Berger, Klaus. "Almosen für Israel." *New Testament Studies* 23 (1977) 180–204.

Best, Ernest. *A Commentary on the First and Second Epistle to the Thessalonians*. London: Adam & Charles Black, 1972.

Betz, Hans Dieter. *Nachfolge und Nachahmung Jesu Christi im Neuen Testament*. Tübingen: Mohr Siebeck, 1967.

———. *Paulus und die sokratische Tradition*. Tübingen: Mohr Siebeck, 1972.

Boers, Hendrikus. "The Form Critical Study of Paul's Letters. 1 Thessalonians as a Case Study." *New Testament Studies* 22 (1976) 140–58.

Boring, M. Eugene. *The Continuing Voice of Jesus. Christian Prophecy and the Gospel Tradition*. Louisville, KY: Westminster John Knox Press, 1991.

Bornkamm, Günther. *Paul*. New York, NY: Harper & Row, 1971.

Borse, Udo. *Der Standort des Galaterbriefes*. Köln: Peter Hanstein, 1972.

Botermann, Helga. *Das Judenedikt des Kaisers Claudius. Römischer Staat und Christiani im 1. Jahrhundert*. Stuttgart: F. Steiner, 1996.

Bowden, Hugh. *Mystery Cults of the Ancient World*. Princeton: Princeton University Press, 2010.

Boyarin, Daniel. *A Radical Jew. Paul and the Politics of Identity*. Berkeley: University of California Press, 1994.

Brocke, Christoph vom. *Thessaloniki—Stadt des Kassander und Gemeinde des Paulus*. Tübingen: Mohr Siebeck, 2001.

Broer, Ingo. "Antijudaismus im Neuen Testament? Versuch einer Annäherung anhand von zwei Texten (1 Thess 2,14 und Mt 27,24f.)" Pp. 321–55 in *Salz der Erde—*

Licht der Welt. Exegetische Studien zum Matthäusevangelium. Festschrift für Anton Vögtle zum 80. Geburtstag. Herausgegeben von Lorenz Oberlinner und Peter Fiedler. Stuttgart: Katholisches Bibelwerk, 1981.

———. "Antisemitismus und Judenpolemik um Neuen Testament. Ein Beitrag zum besseren Verständnis von 1 Thess 2,14–16." *Biblische Notizen* 20 (1983) 59–91.

Bultmann, Rudolf. "Ethische und mystische Religion im Urchristentum." *Die Christliche Welt* 34 (1920) 725–31.

———. *The History of the Synoptic Tradition.* New York: Harper & Row, [2]1968.

———. *Theology of the New Testament.* 2 vols. New York: Charles Scribner's Sons, 1951, 1955.

Chadwick, Henry. "'All Things to All Men' (I Cor. IX. 22)." *New Testament Studies* 1 (1954/55) 261–75.

Charlesworth, James H., ed. *The Old Testament Pseudepigrapha.* Vol. 1, *Apocalyptic Literature and Testaments.* New York, NY: Doubleday & Company, 1983.

Chineira, David Alvarez. *Die Religionspolitik des Kaisers Claudius und die paulinische Mission.* Freiburg: Verlag Herder, 1996.

Conzelmann, Hans. *Gentiles—Jews—Christians. Polemics and Apologetics in the Greco-Roman Era.* Minneapolis, MN: Fortress Press, 1982.

———. *An Outline of the Theology of the New Testament.* New York: Harper & Row, 1969.

———. *Theologie als Schriftauslegung. Aufsätze zum Neuen Testament.* Munich: Chr. Kaiser, 1974.

Corley, Bruce, ed. *Colloquy on New Testament Studies. A Time for Reappraisal and Fresh Approaches.* Macon, GA: Mercer University Press, 1983.

Crossan, John Dominic and Jonathan L. Reed. *In Search of Paul: How Jesus' Apostle Opposed Rome's Empire with God's Kingdom.* San Francisco, CA: Harper, 2004.

Crüsemann, Marlene. *Die pseudepigraphen Briefe an die Gemeinde von Thessaloniki. Studien zu ihrer Abfassung und zur jüdisch-christlichen Sozialgeschichte.* Stuttgart: Kohlhammer, 2010.

Davies, W. D. *Jewish and Pauline Studies.* Philadelphia: Fortress Press, 1984.

Deissmann, Adolf. *Paul: A Study in Social and Religious History.* New York: Harper, 1972 [reprint; 1st ed. 1957].

Dewey, Arthur J., Roy W. Hoover, Lane C. McGaughy, and Daryl D. Schmidt. *The Authentic Letters of Paul. A New Reading of Paul's Rhetoric and Meaning.* Salem, OR: Polebridge Press, 2010.

Dibelius, Martin. *An die Thessalonicher I II. An die Philipper.* Tübingen: Mohr Siebeck, [3]1937.

Dion Chrysostom. *Discourses.* 5 vols. Trans. J. W. Cahoon and H. Lamar Cosby. LCL. 1932–51.

Dobschütz, Ernst von. *Die Thessalonicher-Briefe.* Göttingen: Vandenhoeck & Ruprecht, 1909.

Donfried, Karl Paul. *Paul, Thessalonica, and Early Christianity.* Grand Rapids, MI: Wm. B. Eerdmans Publishing Company, 2002.

Ebel, Eva. *Die Attraktivität frühchristlicher Gemeinden.* Tübingen: Mohr Siebeck, 2004.

Ehrhardt, Arnold A. T.: *Politische Metaphysik von Solon bis Augustin.* Vol. 2. Tübingen: Mohr Siebeck, 1959.

Ehrman, Bart D., ed and trans. *The Apostolic Fathers I.* LCL, 2003.

———. *The New Testament. A Historical Introduction to the Early Christian Writings.* New York: Oxford University Press, [5]2012.

Feldmeier, Reinhard. *The First Letter of Peter.* Waco, TX: Baylor University Press, 2008.

Fitzmyer, John A. T. *First Corinthians. A New Translation with Introduction and Commentary.* New Haven: Yale University Press, 2008.

Frame, James Everett. *A Critical and Exegetical Commentary on the Epistles of St. Paul to the Thessalonians.* New York: Charles Scribner's Sons, 1912.

Funk, Robert W. "The Apostolic *Parousia*: Form and Significance." Pp. 249–68 in *Christian History and Interpretation. Studies Presented to John Knox.* Ed. W. R. Farmer, C. F. D. Moule, and R. Richard Niebuhr. Cambridge: At the University Press, 1967.

———. "The Enigma of the Famine Visit." *Journal of Biblical Literature* 75 (1956) 130–36.

———. and Roy Hoover. *The Five Gospels: The Search for the Authentic Words of Jesus.* New York, NY: MacMillan Publishing Company, 1993.

Furnish, Victor Paul. *1 Thessalonians, 2 Thessalonians.* Nashville, TN: Abingdon Press, 2007.

Georgi, Dieter. *The Opponents of Paul in Second Corinthians.* Philadelphia, PA: Fortress Press, 1986.

———. *Remembering the Poor: The History of Paul's Collection for Jerusalem.* Nashville, PA: Abingdon Press, 1992.

Giesen, Heinz. *Jesu Heilsbotschaft für die Kirche.* Leuven: Peeters, 2004.

Haensch, Rudolf. "Das Statthalterarchiv." *Zeitschrift der Savigny-Stiftung für Rechtsgeschichte* 109 (1992). Romanistische Abteilung. Köln: Böhlau Verlag, 1992: 209–317.

Harnack, Adolf. *The Date of the Acts and of the Synoptic Gospels.* New Testament Studies IV. New York, NY: G. P. Putnam's Sons, 1911.

Harnisch, Wolfgang. *Eschatologische Existenz: Ein exegetischer Beitrag zum Sachanliegen von 1. Thessalonicher 4,13–5,11.* Göttingen: Vandenhoeck & Ruprecht, 1973.

Harrison, James R. *Paul and the Imperial Authorities at Thessalonica and Rome: A Study in the Conflict of Ideology.* Tübingen: Mohr Siebeck, 2004.

Hengel, Martin. *The Zealots. Investigations into the Jewish Freedom Movement in the Period from Herod I until 70 A.D.* Edinburgh: T. & T. Clark, 1989.

———. and Anna Maria Schwemer. *Paul between Damascus and Antioch: The Unknown Years.* Louisville, KY: Westminster John Knox Press, 1997.

Holtz, Traugott. *Der erste Brief an die Thessalonicher.* Zürich: Benziger Verlag, 1986.

Hurd, John C. *The Earlier Letters of Paul—and Other Studies.* Frankfurt: Peter Lang, 1998.

———. Introduction. Pp. 265–70 in *Colloquy on New Testament Studies. A Time for Reappraisal and Fresh Approaches.* Ed. with introduction by Bruce Corley. Macon, GA: Mercer University Press, 1983.

———. *The Origin of I Corinthians.* London: SPCK, 1965.

Hyldahl, Niels. *Die paulinische Chronologie.* Leiden: Brill, 1986.

———. *The History of Early Christianity.* Frankfurt: Peter Lang, 1997.

Jeremias, Joachim. *Unknown Sayings of Jesus.* London: SPCK, [2]1964.

Jewett, Robert. "Chronology and Methodology: Reflections on the Debate over
    Chapters in a Life of Paul." Pp. 271–87 in *Colloquy on New Testament Studies. A
    Time for Reappraisal and Fresh Approaches*. Ed. with introduction by Bruce Corley.
    Macon, GA: Mercer University Press, 1983.
———. *A Chronology of Paul's Life*. Philadelphia: Fortress Press, 1982.
———. *The Thessalonian Correspondence: Pauline Rhetoric and Millenarian Piety*.
    Philadelphia, PA: Fortress Press 1986.
Josephus, Flavius. *Jewish War. Antiquities of the Jews. Life. Against Apion*. Trans. H. St.
    Thackeray, R. Marcus, and L. H. Feldmann. 10 vols. LCL, 1926ff.
Käsemann, Ernst. *New Testament Questions of Today*. London: SCM Press, 1969.
Kampling, Rainer. "Eine auslegungsgeschichtliche Skizze zu 1 Thess 2,14–16." Pp.
    183–213 in *Begegnungen zwischen Christentum und Judentum in Antike und
    Mittelalter. Festschrift für Heinz Schreckenberg*. Herausgegeben von Dietrich-Alex
    Koch und Hermann Lichtenberger. Göttingen: Vandenhoeck & Ruprecht, 1993.
Keck, Leander E. *Romans*. Nashville, TN: Abingdon Press, 2005.
Klassen, William A. "The Sacred Kiss in the New Testament." *New Testament Studies*
    39 (1993) 122–35.
Klein, Günter. "Apokalyptische Naherwartung bei Paulus." In Pp. 241–62. *Neues
    Testament und christliche Existenz. Festschrift für Herbert Braun zum 70. Geburtstag*.
    Ed. Hans Dieter Betz and Luise Schottroff. Tübingen: Mohr Siebeck, 1963.
Knox, John. *Chapters in a Life of Paul*. Nashville, TN: Abingdon Press 1950.
———. *Chapters in a Life of Paul*. Rev. ed. Introduction by Douglas R. A. Hare.
    Macon, GA: Mercer University Press, 1987.
———. "Chapters in a Life of Paul—A Response to Robert Jewett and Gerd
    Luedemann." Pp. 339–64 in *Colloquy on New Testament Studies. A Time for
    Reappraisal and Fresh Approaches*. Ed. with introduction by Bruce Corley. Macon,
    GA: Mercer University Press, 1983.
———. "'Fourteen Years Later'—A Note on the Pauline Chronology." *Journal of
    Religion* 16 (1936) 341–49.
———. *Never Far from Home: The Story of My Life*. Waco, TX: Word Books, 1975.
———. "The Pauline Chronology: Buck-Taylor-Hurd Revisited." Pp. 258–74 in *The
    Conversation Continues: Studies in Paul & John. In Honor of J. Louis Martyn*. Ed.
    Robert T. Fortna and Beverly R. Gaventa. Nashville, TN: Abington Press, 1990.
———. "The Pauline Chronology." *Journal of Biblical Literature* 58 (1939) 15–29.
———. Preface. Pp. xiii–xiv in Gerd Lüdemann. *Paul—Apostle to the Gentiles. Studies
    in Chronology*. Philadelphia, PA: Fortress Press, 1984.
———. "Reflections." Pp. 107–13 in *Cadbury, Knox, and Talbert: American
    Contributions to the Study of Acts*. Ed. Mikeal Parsons and Joseph B. Tyson.
    Atlanta, GA: Scholars Press, 1992.
———. "Rom 15:14–33 and Paul's Apostolic Mission." *Journal of Biblical Literature*
    100 (1964) 1–11.
Koester, Helmut. *History, Culture and Religion of the Hellenistic Age*. Vol. 1.
    Introduction to the New Testament. Berlin: de Gruyter, ²1995.
Konradt, Matthias. *Gericht und Gemeinde: Eine Studie zur Bedeutung und Funktion
    von Gerichtsaussagen im Rahmen der paulinischen Ekklesiologie und Ethik im 1
    Thess und 1 Kor*. Berlin: de Gruyter, 2003.
Lampe, Peter. *From Paul to Valentinus: Christians at Rome in the First Two Centuries*.

Minneapolis, MN: Fortress Press, 2003.

Laub, Franz. *1. und 2. Thessalonicherbrief.* Munich: Kösel, ²1988.

———. *Eschatologische Verkündigung und Lebensgestaltung bei Paulus.* Regensburg: Pustet 1973.

Leon, Harry J. *The Jews of Ancient Rome.* Philadelphia: Jewish Publication Society of America, 1960.

Lindemann, Andreas. "Christliche Gemeinden und das Römische Reich im ersten und im zweiten Jahrhundert." *Wort und Dienst. Jahrbuch der Kirchlichen Hochschule Bethel Neue Folge* 18 (1985) 105–33.

Lohse, Eduard. *Der Brief an die Römer.* Göttingen: Vandenhoeck & Ruprecht, 2003.

———. *Paulus.* München: Beck, 1996. ·

Luckensmeyer, David. *The Eschatology of First Thessalonians.* Göttingen: Vandenhoeck & Ruprecht, 2009.

Lüdemann, Gerd. *The Acts of the Apostles: What Really Happened in the Earliest Days of the Church.* Amherst, NY: Prometheus Books, 2005.

———. "Acts of Impropriety. The Imbalance of History and Theology in Luke-Acts." *Toronto Journal of Theology* 24 (2008) 65–79.

———. *Die ersten drei Jahre Christentum.* Springe: zu Klampen, 2009.

———. "The First Three Years of Christianity." *Toronto Journal of Theology* 25 (2009) 19–40.

———. *Heretics. The Other Side of Christianity.* Louisville, KY: Westminster John Knox Press, 1996.

———. *Jesus after 2000 Years. What He Really Said and Did.* Amherst, NY: Prometheus Books, 2001.

———. "Das Judenedikt des Claudius (Apg 18,2)." Pp. 289–98 in *Der Treue Gottes trauen. Beiträge zum Werk des Lukas.* Ed. Claus Bussmann and Walter Radl. Freiburg: Herder 1991.

———. *Opposition to Paul in Jewish Christianity.* Minneapolis, MN: Fortress Press, 1989.

———. *Paul—Apostle to the Gentiles. Studies in Chronology.* Philadelphia, PA: Fortress Press, 1984.

———. *Paul: The Founder of Christianity.* Amherst, NY: Prometheus Books, 2002.

———. *Primitive Christianity. A Survey of Recent Studies and Some New Proposals.* London: T & T Clark, 2003.

———. *What Jesus Didn't Say.* Salem, OR: Polebridge Press, 2011.

Lünemann, Gottlieb. *Kritisch exegetisches Handbuch über die Briefe an die Thessalonicher.* Göttingen: Vandenhoeck & Ruprecht, ³1867.

Luz, Ulrich. *Das Geschichtsverständnis des Paulus.* Munich: Chr. Kaiser Verlag, 1968.

Lyons, George. *Pauline Autobiography. Toward a New Understanding.* Atlanta, GA: Scholars Press, 1985.

Malherbe, Abraham. *The Letters to the Thessalonians.* New York, NY: Doubleday, 2000.

———. *Moral Exhortation, A Greco-Roman Sourcebook.* Philadelphia, PA: The Westminster Press, 1986.

———. *Paul and the Thessalonians: The Philosophic Tradition of Pastoral Care.* Philadelphia, PA: Fortress Press, 1987.

———. *Paul and the Popular Philosophers.* Minneapolis: Fortress Press, 1989.

Marxsen, Willi. "Auslegung von 1 Thess 4,13–18." *Zeitschrift für Theologie und Kirche* 66 (1969) 22–37.

———. *Der erste Brief an die Thessalonicher.* Zürich: Theologischer Verlag, 1979.

Millar, Fergus. *A Study of Dio Cassius.* Oxford: At the Clarendon Press, 1964.

Minear, Paul S. "The Jerusalem Fund and Pauline Chronology." *Anglican Theological Review* 25 (1943) 389–96.

The Mishnah. Trans. Herbert Danby. Oxford: At the Clarendon Press, 1933.

Mommsen, Theodor. *Judaea und die Juden.* Berlin: Schocken Verlag, 1936.

Munck, Johannes. *Christ and Israel. An Interpretation of Romans 9–11.* Philadelphia: Fortress Press, 1967.

Murphy-O'Connor, Jerome. *A Critical Life of Paul.* New York: Oxford University Press, 1996.

———. *St. Paul's Corinth. Texts and Archaeology.* Collegeville, MN: The Liturgical Press, ³2002.

Nock, Arthur Darby. *St. Paul.* New York, NY: Harper & Row, 1963.

Orosius, Paulus. *Historiae adversum Paganos.* Ed. C. Zangemeister, CSEL 5, 1882.

Pearson, Birger A. "1 Thessalonians 2:13–16: A Deutero-Pauline Interpolation." *Harvard Theological Review* 64 (1971) 79–94.

Räisänen, Heikki. "A Controversial Jew: Paul and his Conflicting Convictions." Pp. 23–37 in *Rediscovering the Apostle Paul.* Ed. Bernhard Brandon Scott. Salem, OR: Polebridge Press, 2011.

Renan, Ernest. *Saint Paul.* New York, NY: G. W. Carleton Publishers, 1869.

Reumann, John. *Philippians. A New Translation with Introduction and Commentary.* New Haven, CT: Yale University Press, 2008.

Richard, Earl J. *First and Second Thessalonians.* Collegeville, MN: The Liturgical Press, 1995.

Riddle, Donald Wayne. *Paul—Man of Conflict.* Nashville, TN: Cokesbury Press, 1940.

Riesner, Rainer. *Paul's Early Period: Chronology, Mission Strategy, Theology.* Grand Rapids, MI: Wm. B. Eerdmans Publishing Company, 1998.

Rigaux, Béda. *The Letters of St. Paul: Modern Studies.* Chicago, IL: Franciscan Herald Press, 1968.

———. *Saint Paul: Les Epîtres aux Thessaloniciens.* Paris: Librairie Lecoffre, 1956.

Rudolph, David J. *A Jew to the Jews. Jewish Contours of Pauline Flexibility in 1 Corinthians 9:13–23.* Tübingen: Mohr Siebeck, 2011.

Sanders, E. P. *Paul.* Oxford: Oxford University Press, 1991.

———. *Paul, the Law, and the Jewish People.* Philadelphia, PA: Fortress Press, 1983.

———. *Paul and Palestinian Judaism: A Comparison of Patterns of Religion.* Philadelphia, PA: Fortress Press, 1977.

Sanders, Jack T. "Paul's 'Autobiographical' Statements in Galatians 1–2." *Journal of Biblical Literature* 85 (1966) 335–43.

Schäfer, Peter. *Judeophobia. Attitudes toward the Jews in the Ancient World.* Cambridge, MA: Harvard University Press, 1997.

Schade, Hans-Heinrich. *Apokalyptische Christologie bei Paulus: Studien zum Zusammenhang von Christologie und Eschatologie in den Paulusbriefen.* Göttingen: Vandenhoeck & Ruprecht, ²1984.

Schaller, Berndt. "Die Rolle des Paulus im Verhältnis zwischen Christen und Juden." Pp. 1–36 in *Between Gospel and Election: Explorations in the Interpretation of Romans 9–11*. Ed. Florian Wilk and J. Ross Wagner. Tübingen: Mohr Siebeck 2010.

Schlier, Heinrich. *Der Apostel und seine Gemeinde: Auslegung des Ersten Briefes an die Thessalonicher*. Freiburg: Herder, [2]1972.

Schlueter, Carol J. *Filling up the Measure: Polemical Hyperbole in 1 Thessalonians 2.14–16*. Sheffield: Sheffield Academic Press 1994.

Schmidt, Daryl D. "1 Thess 2.13–16: Linguistic Evidence for an Interpolation." *Journal of Biblical Literature* 102 (1983) 269–79.

Schreckenberg, Heinz. *Die christlichen Adversus-Judaeos-Texte und ihr literarisches und historisches Umfeld (1.–11. Jh.)*. Frankfurt: Peter Lang, 1982.

Schubert, Paul. *Form and Function of the Pauline Thanksgivings*. Berlin: Alfred Töpelmann, 1939.

Schürer, Emil. *The History of the Jewish People in the Age of Jesus Christ (175 B.C.– A.D. 135)*. Vol. III. Part 1, Edinburgh: T & T Clark LTD, 1986.

Scott, James M. "Paul's Use of Deuteronomic Tradition." *Journal of Biblical Literature* 112 (1993) 645–65.

Segal, Alan F. *Paul the Convert: The Apostolate and Apostasy of Saul the Pharisee*. New Haven: Yale University Press, 1990.

Siber, Peter. *Mit Christus leben. Eine Studien zur paulinischen Auferstehungshoffnung*. Zurich: Theologischer Verlag, 1971.

Slingerland, H. Dixon. *Claudian Policy Making and the Early Imperial Repression of Judaism at Rome*. Atlanta, GA: Scholars Press, 1997.

Smith, Abraham. *Comfort One Another. Reconstructing the Rhetoric and Audience of 1 Thessalonians*. Louisville, KY: Westminster John Knox Press, 1995.

Söding, Thomas. *Die Trias Glaube, Liebe, Hoffnung bei Paulus*. Stuttgart: Katholisches Bibelwerk, 1992.

Stambaugh, John E. and David L. Balch. *The New Testament in Its Social Environment*. Philadelphia, PA: The Westminster Press, 1986.

Steck, Odil Hannes. *Israel und das gewaltsame Geschick der Propheten. Untersuchungen zur Überlieferung des deuteronomistischen Geschichtsbildes im Alten Testament, Spätjudentum und Urchristentum*. Neukirchen-Vluyn: Neukirchener Verlag, 1967.

Stowers, Stanley K. *The Diatribe and Paul's Letter to the Romans*. Chico: Scholars' Press, 1981.

Strecker, Georg. *Theology of the New Testament*. Louisville, KY: Westminster John Knox Press, 2000.

Suetonius. *The Lives of the Caesars*. Trans. J. C. Rolfe. LCL, 1965.

Suggs, M. J. "Concerning the Date of Paul's Macedonian Ministry." *Novum Testamentum* 4 (1960) 60–68.

Suhl, Alfred. *Paulus und seine Briefe. Ein Beitrag zur paulinischen Chronologie*. Gütersloh: Gerd Mohn, 1975.

Tacitus. *Annals* and *Histories*. 4 vols. Trans. John Jackson and Clifford H. Moore. LCL, 1931–37.

Talbert, Charles H. *Reading Luke-Acts in its Mediterranean Milieu*. Leiden: Brill, 2003.

Tatum, Gregory, O.P. *New Chapters in the Life of Paul. The Relative Chronology of His Career.* Washington, DC: The Catholic Biblical Association of America, 2006.

Taubes, Jacob. *The Political Theology of Paul.* Stanford, CA: Stanford University Press, 2004.

Versnel, Henk S. "Making Sense of Jesus' Death. The Pagan Contribution." Pp. 213–94 in *Deutungen des Todes Jesu im Neuen Testament.* Herausgegben von Jörg Frey und Jens Schröder. Tübingen: Mohr Siebeck, 2005.

Volz, Paul. *Die Eschatologie der jüdischen Gemeinde im neutestamentlichen Zeitalter.* Tübingen: Mohr Siebeck, 1910.

Welborn, L. L. "Paul's Flight from Damascus: Sources and Evidence for an Historical Evaluation." Pp. 41–60 in *Historische Wahrheit und theologische Wissenschaft. Gerd Lüdemann zum 50. Geburtstag.* Ed. Alf Özen. Frankfurt: Peter Lang, 1996.

Wendland, Paul. *Die hellenistisch-römische Kultur in ihren Beziehungen zu Judentum und Christentum.* Tübingen: Mohr Siebeck, 1912.

Woodman, A. J. *Tacitus. The Annals.* Translated with Introduction and Notes. Indianapolis, IN: Hackett Publishing Company, 2004.

Wrede, William. *Die Echtheit des zweiten Thessalonicherbriefs untersucht.* Leipzig: J. C. Hinrichssche Buchhandlung 1903.

———. *Paul.* Boston, MA: American Unitarian Association, 1908.

Zeller, Dieter. *Christus unter den Göttern.* Stuttgart: Verlag Katholisches Bibelwerk, 1993.

Index of Passages

Index of Authors
and Subjects

About the Author

Gerd Lüdemann is Professor Emeritus of the History and Literature of Early Christianity, and Founder of the Archive "Religionsgeschichtliche Schule" at the University of Göttingen, Germany. He is also a Visiting Scholar at Vanderbilt Divinity School in Nashville, Tennessee, a Fellow of the Jesus Seminar, and has served as cochair of the Society of Biblical Literature Seminar on Jewish Christianity. He is the author of many books including, *The Unholy in Holy Scripture* (1997), *The Great Deception* (1999), *Paul: The Founder of Christianity* (2002), *The Resurrection of Christ* (2004), *The Acts of the Apostles* (2005), *Intolerance and the Gospel* (2007), *Eyes That See Not: The Pope Looks at Jesus* (2008) and *What Jesus Didn't Say* (2011).

Lightning Source UK Ltd.
Milton Keynes UK
UKHW021415240220
359232UK00007B/559